In Water and in Blood

In Water and in Blood

A Spirituality of Solidarity and Hope

Robert J. Schreiter

CROSSROAD · NEW YORK

1988

The Crossroad Publishing Company
370 Lexington Avenue, New York, N.Y. 10017

Printed in the United States of America

Library of Congress Cataloging-in-Publication Data

Schreiter, Robert J.
   In water and in blood : a spirituality of solidarity and hope /
Robert Schreiter.
   p. cm.
   ISBN 0-8245-0877-7 (pbk.)
   1. Precious Blood, Devotion to. 2. Revolutions—Religious
aspects—Catholic Church. 3. Spirituality—Catholic Church.
   4. Latin America—Church history—20th century. 5. Catholic Church-
-Doctrines—History. I. Title.
BX2159.P7S37   1988
248—dc19   88-2727
                                                   CIP

Jesus Christ it is who came through water and blood,
  not in water only, but in water and in blood.
It is the Spirit who testifies to this,
  and the Spirit is truth.
Thus there are three that testify,
  the Spirit, and the water, and the blood—
  and these three are of one accord. (1 Jn. 5:6–8)

To the men and women who follow a spirituality of the blood of Christ, building community and facing conflict, in hopes for a better world.

Contents

Introduction

WHY A SPIRITUALITY OF THE BLOOD OF CHRIST?

This book aims at developing the outlines of a contemporary spirituality based on the biblical image of the blood of Christ. This image has a long history in Christianity. In the patristic period, it was used especially to communicate values surrounding God's redeeming forgiveness in Jesus Christ, the eucharist, and martyrdom. In the Western Middle Ages, it came again to the forefront in devotion to the passion of Christ and to the eucharist, as well as in a special mystical theology of union with the Lord. The eighteenth and nineteenth centuries witnessed a resurgence of interest in the image, in pietisms of both Catholic and Protestant stripe, mainly to communicate God's abounding love for the sinner.

It is indeed through this latter development that most Christians are familiar with the notion of the blood of Christ today. For many Catholics, it seems tied to an older theology having to do with the application of merits gained in the death of Christ, something that no longer gives adequate expression to our understanding of relationship with God in grace. It also seems inexorably bound up with the ornate and often sentimental rhetoric so favored in nineteenth-century piety, thereby having a genuinely alienating effect on contemporary sensibilities. For many Protestants, language about the blood of Christ seems to have been taken over entirely by conservative groups trying to reawaken an earlier pietism. Concentration either upon the gore of death or apocalyptic expectation only heightens aversion to talk about the redeeming power of Christ's blood.

And for still others, the collapse of the devotional fabric of liberal Western Christianity, especially in its Catholic varieties, took with it devotion to the blood of Christ in its descent. To concentrate too much on this image threatens to disrupt efforts at an integrated spirituality, rather than provide a cohesive center for it.

So why a book on the spirituality of the blood of Christ? A number of factors have converged to make a reexamination of this ancient tradition feasible.

Perhaps the most important is a resurgence of interest in this image in Latin America. Under the strain of social and political conflict, many Christians in that part of the world have been turning to this old image, but in a new way. Rather than stressing God's love, or contemplating the blood of Christ to arouse compunction in the heart of the sinner (both, of course, legitimate approaches), men and women in Latin America have found in the blood of Christ a way of dealing with their own suffering. They are finding in it a key to Christ's solidarity with those who suffer and a hope that their suffering, too, can somehow be redemptive in their situations. A spirituality of the blood of Christ, then, contains a message about the bonding of the human community, and a hope that reaches beyond the apparent hopelessness of the current situation.

Finding in Christ's suffering a paradigm for enduring our own is not a new idea; it certainly motivated the martyrs of the early church and much of the devotion to the passion of Christ in the Middle Ages. What is new here is a more conscious application of these insights to situations of conflict, and to the concomitant need to keep building up the bonds of human community. These two themes—conflict and community—will emerge over and over again in the pages to follow.

In pursuing this new angle of entry into the meaning of the blood of Christ for contemporary Christians, there has also been a concern to explore more closely the biblical foundations of such a spirituality. There has been a feeling that centuries of devotion have encrusted the biblical insights in a dense cover bespeaking cultural situations not shared by contemporary men and women in their cultures today. Jansenism and the sterilities of eighteenth-century Protestant orthodoxies are no longer the obstacles to be overcome. Situations and anthropologies change. Hence there is a need to return to the sources, and to reread the scriptures with the questions of our own time and place.

To be sure, the message that emerges from reflection on the scriptures continues to be refracted through the cultural lens of the reader. My own experience in exploring these themes has been that Central and Latin Americans give more emphasis to resources for conflictual situations, whereas North Americans and Western Europeans focus upon issues of community and alienation. It is not a situation of either-or; both are necessary and both are needed. Their interaction can enrich the entire body of the church.

This book, then, is intended as the beginning of a retrieval of a biblically based spirituality of the blood of Christ. It is concerned with the potential of such a spirituality for undergirding a Christian life committed to a building up of community and for dealing with situations of conflict. The book attempts to do this by a series of explorations of biblical texts and themes that seem especially suited to serve as continuing resources for a contemporary spirituality. An Epilogue highlights some of the insights gained from these explorations and suggests an outline for such a spirituality.

The idea of writing this book began with an invitation to give a series of lectures on this theme in Chile in January 1986. Seven of the twelve chapters had their origins in those lectures. Two versions of those lectures were given in Chile: one set for a gathering of four religious institutes with devotion to the blood of Christ marking their foundation, charisma, and history; and a second set for a wider audience, focusing especially on situations of conflict. The first set was repeated, with some modifications, for a retreat in Peru in 1987.

Those presentations have been reworked for this book, and five new ones added. The Epilogue had its origin in a paper read at a conference in Rome in October 1986. It, too, has been entirely rewritten for this volume.

Many persons deserve my thanks for the insights and efforts they have shared in the course of the writing of this book. Thanks must go first to the Secretariado de la Unión de Sangre de Cristo in Santiago for the invitation that gave rise to this work. In addition, those who gathered in Punta de Tralca and Santiago in Chile, and Chaclacayo in Peru, contributed more than they may have realized. Extended discussions with Barry Fischer and Dennis Kinderman, both confreres of mine in the Society of the Precious Blood, helped polish some of the thought; they also shared with me their own work on similar projects. Anton Loipfinger and John Kalicky, Moderator General and Provincial of the Society, respectively, provided abiding encouragement on this project, for which I am grateful. And Mark Yates and Lac Pham, students in the Society, provided important technical assistance at crucial steps along the way.

I experienced far more the "community" than the "conflict" side of spirituality in working with all of these persons. And for that reason this book is dedicated to them: the men and women who have made the blood of Christ the center of their spirituality as they strive to build up community in a broken world, and as they struggle for justice and live in hope.

Catholic Theological Union   *Robert J. Schreiter, C.PP.S.*
Chicago

Let this Blood Be a Sign to You

Moses called all the elders of Israel and said to them, "Go and procure lambs for your families, and slaughter them as Passover victims. Then take a bunch of hyssop, and dipping it in the blood that is in the basin, sprinkle the lintel and the two doorposts with this blood. But none of you shall go outdoors until morning. For the Lord will go by, striking down the Egyptians. Seeing the blood on the lintel and the two door-posts, the Lord will pass over that door and not let the destroyer come into your houses to strike you down." (Ex. 12:21–23)

This familiar passage from the Book of Exodus has gripped generations of believers, both Jewish and Christian. On one level, the sheer dramatic flow of the story draws the reader into its powerful motifs. An enslaved people is rescued in the darkness of night by the blood of a lamb. As they huddle inside their homes, the destroyer moves through their neighborhoods and the surrounding countryside, leaving death and destruction in his wake. But the doors marked with blood are spared this fate, and are passed by. Those who dwell behind those doors are safe, but the rest of the land experiences the anguish of losing its firstborn. This story of rescue and protection would be told and retold year after year, a story reminding Israel and other oppressed peoples of the danger that haunted their past and the great care that God can show.

But this story of the blood on the doorposts has a second level of meaning, apart from its utter dramatic power. This is the first story in the Pentateuch where a blood ritual is prescribed in such de-tail—that is, the use of blood as a sign or medium for communicating between Israel and God. Blood, the very substance of life—but also a sign of violence and death—becomes the pathway of communication between God and Israel, between Israel and God. And in the subsequent history of Israel, the blood ritual was to become the preeminent way Israel had of communicating with God, and was to be enacted on all important occasions. Blood itself conveys seriousness—blood can somehow carry messages to God about matters of life and death. Although Israel had other means for communication in its sacrifices (incense, grain, first fruits), all really important matters were conveyed with blood. Hence, this first evidence of a blood ritual of this nature is of special importance.

But the story has yet a third level of meaning. This story of God's protecting the Hebrews brings together in a marvelous fashion nearly all the themes of a spirituality of blood found in the Bible. In some ways, this passage from Exodus is like an overture to a musical composition: it presents the motifs and melodies that will thread their way through the entire drama of salvation.

This first chapter, then, will be something of an overture to what will follow. It will explore those bold and simple themes that this Passover story presents. In so doing, these motifs start us on the way through the scriptures in the quest for the biblical resources for a spirituality of blood.

Background to the Passover Story

This blood ritual seems to have been an ancient one in Egypt, older even than the story presented here. It was held at the beginning of the new year, which was celebrated in Egypt with the coming of spring. The transition from winter to spring was considered perilous, a sort of crack running through time, threatening to halt the move from the darkness and deadness of winter to the growing light and vitality of spring. It was dangerous because the forces of death that had accumulated in the darkness of winter (called in the story "the destroyer"), poised as they were on the edge of winter, were always seeking an opportunity to engulf the fragile forces of life coming to birth in the spring. Special protection was necessary for living beings—both human and animal—at this most dangerous of times.

Egyptians protected themselves from the destroyer by anointing the doorways of their houses with blood. Blood was believed to contain special properties of protection. Throughout the East Mediterranean region, it was believed that the very life-force of an animal or a human was located in the blood. And that life-force was not the possession of the individual, but was given for a time to each mortal by God, the seat of all life. Thus blood on the doorpost of the house meant that the life within belonged to God, and any destroyer who wished to snatch it away had to contend with God.

At the same time, however, that sign of life was a mark of death. For blood that had been shed was blood out of place, no longer sustaining the life of an animal or a human. Blood shed became a sign of both violence and death, a fearful and terrible thing. For blood shed speaks of the naked power of God, which no creature can escape; it speaks of death, from which no one can hope to return. It speaks, too, of the marauding power of violence and evil, which tears up the fragile fabric of human life and community.

Thus the blood on the doorpost carried a message of both protection and warning, an affirmation of life and an acknowledgment of the reality and violence of death. This was heightened by the fact that, in this ritual, the blood had to come from an animal that had not yet reached maturity. It was the blood of an innocent, the blood of an animal that had not yet reached the full measure of strength, the blood of one still at the most lively stage of existence. To use the blood of a young lamb only emphasized all the more strongly the contrast between life and death, because the most lively one, the furthest removed from the decay of old age, experiences the violence of premature death. To take blood from such a creature only emphasized the more the struggle between life and death that the season portended.

And so the Egyptians anointed the entry to their homes with youthful blood as a way of protecting themselves as winter made its perilous and unsure way into spring. The Hebrews in Egypt probably practiced this ritual as well while they were there (or perhaps brought a similar ritual with them in their wanderings into Egypt; see Ex. 5:3). And when they joined the other tribes to form Israel at Schechem (Jos. 24:1–28), they brought with them this ritual as a way of remembering how God had protected them. The ritual and the accompanying story were to become central to Israel's identity, especially after the return from the exile and the restoration of ritual with the building of the second temple at the time of Ezra. It bespoke something fundamental about Israel's relationship to God.

Motifs in an Overture

With this background on the ritual, I can now turn to some of the themes found in this story. As was noted above, these recur

throughout the scriptures and are therefore basic to any spirituality of the blood of Christ. Here they signal beginnings that will
shape the experience of God's people. Four themes will be explored
here:

1. the boundary between life and death;
2. protection from the destroyer;
3. the blood of an innocent lamb;
4. a seal and a witness.

The Boundary between Life and Death

As was noted in the description of the Egyptian blood ritual, the
reason why blood plays such an important role in communicating
with forces stronger than ourselves (in this case, both God and the
destroyer) is because it holds together within itself the mysteries of
life and death. Blood is the vehicle of life; its spilling presages
death. Thus blood represents those points where life and death
meet. And that meeting is seldom a harmonious one. It is more like
the points where two geological plates clash in the earth—the
focus of an earthquake. Enormous tension is always present, for
neither side wants to move for the sake of the other.

A spirituality that takes blood as its central symbol is a spirituality that dwells on those points where life and death face each
other, where struggle is always going on. The blood rituals of Israel
all have an awareness of that line as part of them. In the Passover
story, the blood marks the threshold of the house, the line the
destroyer may not cross. In the expiatory rites, the blood of the
victim will mark the line where sin is stopped from engulfing the
people. In the covenant rite, the blood draws a line of God's protection around a people in a hostile wilderness. In all of these, the
blood clearly demarcates the frontier between life and death.

That blood should become such a strong symbol for Israel is not
surprising. For Israel came to know God as a God who rescues, as a
God who takes sides with those pushed to the margins of society:
the poor, the widowed, the orphaned, those who do not receive
justice, those considered nonpersons in their own society. And
later, Jesus' own ministry reaffirmed that experience of God: those
who were being pushed to the edges of society at that time felt
welcomed by Jesus. Indeed, in his proclamation of the reign of

God, Jesus recast those lines of life and death in society, making those who had dwelt on the edges now the center of God's reign.

A spirituality of blood is a spirituality that seeks out those who live on the margins of society and chooses to dwell with them. It does this because there the struggle between the forces of life and death is at its most acute, and there the divine presence of life is most urgently needed. Blood is such a strong symbol of that presence because it is a symbol of the mystery of life and the mystery of death. As a symbol of the mystery of life, it protects the families of the Hebrews in the Passover story. (It is significant that the Hebrews are told to gather as families, or to join a family if they found themselves alone. It is the family—not the individual—that is here considered the basic unit of life.

But it is at the same time a symbol of all that is not life and is beyond life—a symbol of violence, of evil, of death, of supernatural power. That is why it takes up its dwelling at the point where life and death meet. In embracing both life and death, it may be the only thing that can keep the boundary between life and death from opening up as a great abyss. It may be the only thing strong enough to keep us from plunging into that great emptiness.

As we come to understand this aspect of Israel's spirituality and what it means for our own time, we need to ask where those boundaries between life and death are being drawn today. Does that boundary cut through families where communication has broken down? Is it evident in the seemingly unreconcilable political differences that threaten to erupt in civil war? Does it divide the haves and the have-nots of a society? It is at those points of tension and conflict where those who follow a spirituality of blood are called especially to be. And one of the first steps toward developing a spirituality of the blood of Christ is to discover where those lines run through our own lives, our families, and our society.

Protection from the Destroyer

Israel came to know God as a God who saves. The word "salvation" has many meanings, and in the course of the development of the people of God it came to include many factors. But one meaning surfaces most clearly in the Passover story. Here God's salvation means protection: the blood of the lamb means protection from the destroyer.

When most persons use the word "salvation" they tend to think of something already fully completed. Thus, our sins are truly forgiven, we are clearly lifted out of oppression, we achieve genuine liberty. But when we examine the scriptures and our own experience more closely, we discover that salvation is usually less than complete. Our sin is truly forgiven, but we sin again. We overcome one form of oppression only to get enmeshed in another. We free ourselves but fall into new entanglements. We are saved for a time, but then danger threatens us again.

In the Passover story, salvation is very limited. It is not even salvation in a full sense; it is simply protection for one night. The destroyer continues to threaten, but the Hebrews are spared for now. They are not necessarily a better people, but they are at least safe. And sometimes that is all that salvation can be.

As we explore how salvation comes to us today, we have to accept the fact that a little protection is often all that can be expected. And often that little protection lasts no more than a night. We protect what we cannot liberate; we survive when we cannot enjoy life in its fullness. When persons find themselves up against the boundary between life and death, when the prospect of living becomes an overwhelming task, the best response is to begin with small steps: take one day at a time. When someone loses the spouse of a lifetime, when someone discovers that he or she has a terminal disease, when one confronts the racism that the majority do not even recognize, when there seems no chance to build a free and just society, when the young find no hope for the future—in all these circumstances crisscrossing our lives, we need to be able to identify fleeting moments of salvation. They are far from total, but they are real nonetheless. They dare not be mistaken for the fullness of salvation, and should not keep us from the struggle to help bring about a fuller life, a more just society. But God sometimes speaks in the gentle breeze rather than the raging storm. And part of what we need to do is to identify and celebrate brief moments of salvation and protection. Just as the Hebrews celebrated the Passover meal while the destroyer circled around them, so we, too, must not let ourselves be robbed of those little moments when the bigger moments seem still so far away.

The blood on the doorposts gave protection. That blood was a sign of both life and death, itself evocative of the tension that continues. By acknowledging the struggle and the conflictual nature of a situation, the first step is made to keep from being swallowed up by it. By acknowledging the struggle directly, blood becomes a reminder to those engaged in struggle—be it a personal one to reconstruct a life or a communal one to rebuild society—that the struggle of life and death will continue to be with us. And in the blood of Christ Christians know that it will someday be overcome.

The Blood of an Innocent Lamb

It is the blood of a young, immature, and innocent lamb that protects the Hebrews from the destroyer. The young, the naive, and the immature protect the adult, the experienced, the shrewd. This is a reversal of what might have been expected: the least likely shield against the destroyer offers the greatest protection.

The God who favors those on the margins of society also favors the powerless and the poor. And because God stands in a special way with them, their strength can indeed be remarkable. It seems as though the power of life becomes more concentrated along that boundary line with death, that the continual awareness of the presence of violence and death heightens the appetite for life. Learning to be without power causes one to come to rely more on the power that comes from God, rather than from one's own resources. By having to rely on the power of God one can come to understand better the depth of one's own powerlessness. Thus the weakness of the young lamb foreshadows the ways in which God will become manifest more clearly among the weak, the unfavored, and the poor. The blood, the life-force of the lamb, exhibits in a special way the fragility and the weakness of the creature. It is a life-force that carries within itself a message about needing help to face the acts of violence and death that stalk our lives.

But the blood here is not only the blood of the powerless and the weak, it is the blood of the innocent. The lamb in no way deserves to die; it has not reached maturity, and it has done nothing wrong. Yet its innocence must face destructiveness and evil. This opens up another aspect of a spirituality of blood: the suffering of the innocent. Suffering is seldom fair or just, but is always particularly unfair and unjust when the innocent are afflicted. And all too often suffering does come to the innocent in illness and accident, through racial and economic discrimination, through the denial of human rights. The wrenching pain of the suffering of the innocent threatens not only the sufferer, but calls into question all our fundamental beliefs about the goodness and the fairness of the world.

Yet throughout the scriptures there is a record of how the suffering of the innocent is especially redemptive, is uncommonly strong in the face of evil. The suffering servant songs of the Book of Isaiah are a testimony to this. And it is in Jesus, the one without sin, that this clash of innocence with evil reaches its highest pitch.

The blood of the innocent cries out—from the blood of Abel to the blood of political prisoners tortured today and to the aborted. The blood of those who die prematurely from exhaustion, from hunger, and from despair keeps us in mind of the deep contradictions that mark our world. And it is a spirituality of the redeeming blood of Christ that keeps us from being immobilized by our own rage, or succumbing to despair in the face of those contradictions. The blood that has been shed keeps us close to the stark reality; the blood that redeems nourishes our hope.

A Seal and a Witness

In the Passover story, the blood is not offered in a secret ritual; it is spread in broad strokes on the very entry to the house. It becomes a sign to God and to the destroyer. It witnesses to those who dwell within, who are making themselves one with the blood through the eating of the lamb's flesh.

The blood that is used for the sign is blood that has been shed. It is a sign that those who put it there on the lintel and the doorposts know what the struggle of life and death is all about. They have felt that contest between the forces of life and death in their own bodies; they have known suffering. By placing the blood of the innocent lamb on the doorpost, they have identified themselves with a God who sides with the innocent sufferer. They witness to their allegiance to that God and to a solidarity with those whom God calls a special people. That blood becomes at once a seal of their solidarity with that God and with those who suffer, as well as a witness to God saving, even now. That is why Israel came to repeat the Passover meal each year, to reassert its bond with this saving God and to witness to that God's continuing fidelity.

Throughout the course of the scriptures, the sign of blood draws attention to this struggle, from the covenant in the Sinai wilderness to the one hundred forty-four thousand sealed in the Book of

Revelation. The blood on the cross of Christ becomes the great seal of God's commitment to us and a witness to a redemption of suffering. It becomes a sign of solidarity in confrontation with the forces of the destroyer. And those who follow a spirituality of the blood are called to join in that solidarity against the destroyer, to witness to the saving power of God, made manifest in a special way among those bereft of power and resources.

An overture gives only a taste of what will follow. It sets out themes in broad strokes. Four such themes were explored here, themes that will recur in many variations in the drama of a God who protects and saves. "Let this blood be a sign to you": a sign of the enormous power of life when it is threatened by death, a sign of standing by those who suffer. It is a proclamation of how God deals with the world, and a pledge that injustice and isolation will be overcome.

The Blood that Holds the World Together

Moses took half of the blood and put it in large bowls; the other half he splashed on the altar. Taking the book of the covenant, he read aloud to the people, who answered, "All that the Lord has said we will heed and do." Then he took the blood and sprinkled it on the people, saying, "This is the blood of the covenant which the Lord has made with you in accordance with all these words of his." (Ex. 24:6–8)

This passage from Exodus presents another dramatic scene from the life of the Hebrew people. Moses has led a band of slaves in revolt out of Egypt. They had been foreigners in that land, and had been pressed into servitude by the Egyptians. Huddled now in the desert, they bear many of the marks of an oppressed people. They do not have much sense of self-worth; they have been told for so long that they could only be slaves that they find it hard to picture themselves in any other way. Yet the small flame of liberty has not gone out completely: they have chosen to go into the dangerous and uncertain world of the desert rather than stay in a civilized Egypt where they were not free. But they are finding it hard to live as a free people. They have no experience of this, and some even want to go back to the security of their former state.

And then God gives them a law, a way of organizing themselves into a people, a new way of being, something very different from servitude. But there is more. God makes a treaty, a covenant, with them. If they follow the law, they become God's own people and will come to belong to God in a very special and distinctive way. They will have an identity, and a sense of pride and self-worth.

This covenant is then sealed in a blood ritual, a blood sacrifice. Young bulls are killed, and their blood is collected in large bowls.

Half the blood is splashed on the altar and the other half is sprinkled on the people. Moses then proclaims that God's covenant is in force.

Sacrifice as Communication

This seemingly simple ritual is in fact a very complex one, and deserves closer attention. Understanding this ritual better will help to appreciate the language of sacrifice that will be found later in the scriptures.

For this blood ritual is a sacrifice, one of the many forms of sacrifice spoken of in the Hebrew scriptures (peace offerings, offerings of thanksgiving, sin offerings, expiatory sacrifices). And in the New Testament, the death of Christ will be seen as a sacrifice. Catholic traditions hold that the celebration of the eucharist is a sacrifice, renewing the sacrifice of Jesus. Hence it is worthwhile to examine more closely the meaning of this concept.

Most persons today have very little understanding of sacrifice. If someone were to ask the average person what sacrifice is, the answer would probably be: "It means to give something up." And if pressed further to identify what makes this ritual in Exodus 24 a sacrifice, the answer would probably be: "The killing of the bulls." Sacrifice is identified either with giving something up, or with what would be considered by many rather crude and barbaric rituals involving the slaughter of animals.

Giving something up and the killing of animals are indeed part of what sacrifice means. But that is only a small part, and does not encompass the entire meaning. The word "sacrifice" comes from two Latin words, meaning "to make something sacred" or "to do the sacred thing." Sacrifice is really about communication, and specifically about communication with God. It is a way of bridging the great chasm between our world and the world of God. Sacrifice tries to speak where human words do not reach far enough. Sacrifice is a way of reaching out into the unseen world where God dwells. And it tries to express deep human emotions and yearnings that cannot be voiced easily. Sacrifice, then, has to do with communication.

A sacrificial ritual generally has three parts. The first part is the offering. What is offered has to stand for or represent those who make the offering. It must come out of the substance of the offerers, not out of their surplus. That is why firstfruits and the firstborn of the herd were often offered, for these represented the totality of what one hoped to receive. Moreover, the offering was always to be whole and unblemished, not something one planned to dispose of anyway. The offering, which will cross over into the world of the divine, had to be as representative as possible of those making the offering, because the offering was the bearer of the communication to the world of God. It crosses the boundary that separates this world from the supernatural world.

The second part of sacrifice is the transformation of the offering. The moment of transformation is the moment of passing over the boundary between the two worlds. That transformation was usually brought about by the destruction of the offering, either slaughtering the animal or burning the grain offering. The destruction has two meanings. First of all, by destroying the offering, it passes out of the offerer's possession irrevocably—it cannot be reclaimed. And secondly, the death or destruction of the offering signifies that it has passed over into the supernatural world, where the dead dwell, and where no mortal may go with hopes of ever returning.

In the third part of sacrifice, communion takes place. The offering passes back to this world. It crosses that boundary between the two worlds, but now imbued with the world of the divine. The meat of the slaughtered animal is shared with those who have made the offering. The sharing of animal flesh is paralleled by the sharing of the spirit of the animal in the supernatural world. In this way, the world of humanity and the world of God are united. Communication and communion take place, and this world is strengthened and renewed by its contact with God.

In this particular story from Exodus, the blood is carefully collected into bowls at the time of the killing of the bulls. Those large bowls of steaming blood create a mysterious kind of presence, as though God is present there in the vapors arising from the vats. It is as though the blood were still alive, still suffused with life-force, even though the animals are clearly dead.

Moses then flings half of the blood against the altar, emphasizing thereby that the message is carried to God. The other half is sprinkled on the people, which says that the message returns from God. And the message is that this band of slaves is now constituted as a people—and not just any people, but God's special people.

The dramatic gestures of this ritual, in which a people addresses God through the blood, and the unseen God addresses the people through that same blood, create a powerful cycle of communication. As part of the force of life, the blood creates new life, making slaves into free people. Those who had been pushed to the margins are now brought to the center of things by God.

In the Passover story, a blood ritual protected the people by fending off the destroyer. Protection from harm and danger was a key aspect of the spirituality of blood that emerges from reflection on that event. In the Exodus 24 story, the theme is life: life as new possibilities, a fresh start, the energy for giving life a new meaning. The blood here, in being divided out among the people, ends their scattered existence, and gives them new cohesion and power. Blood poured out recalls sapped strength and death. But in this story it also symbolizes participation in the life-force of God.

Four aspects of this story illustrate blood as the promise of life and offer resources for a spirituality of blood:

1. it takes place in the desert;
2. it celebrates the rule of law;
3. a band of slaves becomes a people;
4. the blood bond holds the world together.

In the Desert

It is significant that God speaks through the blood ritual in the desert. The Hebrews find themselves in a wilderness outside human society and civilization. The Sinai wilderness is a desert: the ordinary daily needs of food, water, and shelter become repeated and major preoccupations. For one does not live in a desert; one only survives there.

And so we have an already marginated people reduced even further by being pushed into the most marginal of situations. By having to deal almost constantly with survival (as so much of the Exodus narrative describes), the basic boundary between life and death becomes even more prominent in their awareness. There is no buffer to shield them from the stark realities of living and dying. The strain of having to concentrate on survival all the time can go hard on one's sense of self-worth and dignity. When this happens to a people already marginated, its effect can be devastating.

It is in this context that the blood ritual takes place. Those steaming bowls of blood, the splashing of blood on the altar and the people speaks loudly of the struggle between life and death, the war between cosmic forces in the silence of the desert. Both the fragility and the power of life echo in that splashing of blood. It is as though only blood can say what needs to be said in an area where usually only the wind and the howls of predatory animals are heard.

A spirituality of blood speaks with special eloquence in the desert, among a people severely marginated. Things others may take for granted do not come easily to those who are poor, who are refugees, who are imprisoned. Sheer survival becomes the main preoccupation. A spirituality of blood proclaims life in a world where death seems to have the upper hand. But its proclamation is not superficial, like telling the hungry to be well fed, or telling the imprisoned to experience freedom. It is not a proclamation that the comfortable can make to those without comfort. Rather, this spirituality wells up in the very midst of the poor and the marginated. It is always a proclamation with, rather than for, the marginated. It gives shape and hope to the struggles of a people.

The desert makes many things clear. It does not allow for easy compromise. As a land of death, it provides a dramatic setting for the blood ritual of life. Those who follow a spirituality of blood proclaim this stark contrast by announcing life where death seems to have taken the high ground. In service to those who have been declared nonpersons by society—the abandoned, the imprisoned, the refugees, the strangers, the homeless—the message of the blood is clear: the desert will not prevail. Blood calls to life through the special care of a God who leads them out of the desert to a new and promised land. Blood proclaims life and hope beyond the perils of the wilderness. It offers the vision of a new existence and affirms a basic human dignity when everything else seems to deny it. It echoes hope in the silent void of the desert. And that message of hope, proclaiming a word of life in the silence of death, continues down into all the desert situations of our own time.

Celebration of the Rule of Law

The blood ritual that Moses enacted in the desert was not in-tended to communicate some abstract message about life in general. As the story tells it, in the middle of the ritual, Moses read the people the whole book of the law, the ordinances by which they were to live and relate to one another. The law gave the people a way out of the desert, a way to keep from sinking to a less than human way of being together. And after the Hebrews gave their assent to the law, Moses confirmed and sealed them in that way of living with the blood.

Christians often disparage the Mosaic law, saying that it is utterly surpassed in the gospel freedom given in Jesus Christ. Law and freedom are set against each other, as though the law represented a form of bondage that kept a people from realizing its true dignity. But such an understanding is really quite superficial, and misinterprets both the meaning of the law and the biblical understanding of it. Moreover, many North Americans and West Europeans growing up in situations where there is protection from arbitrary and lawless behavior may not appreciate how important law is both to individuals and to society.

It is perhaps only in situations where laws and conventional patterns and rhythms of society have broken down or are perversely skewed that it becomes clear what a law can mean for a people. Likewise, those who work with persons who have suffered severe emotional trauma or breakdown know how important it is to be able to participate again in the simplest of human routines. Basic human interactions—returning a greeting, eating together, encountering strangers—become monumental achievements. Those who have been forcibly isolated, put into solitary confinement, or tortured, can find the most elementary patterns of social interaction—receiving food, engaging in conversation—almost beyond their ability.

And on a larger scale, when a people is denied the rule of law, the importance of law becomes more strikingly evident. When normal human movement is restricted by house arrest and curfew, when individuals are seized arbitrarily and "disappear," when homes are invaded and violated by intruders acting on behalf of some self-proclaimed "legitimate" government, when death squads prowl the countryside wreaking their own brand of "justice"—then the value of law takes on a sharp profile. More subtly but often with similar emotional pain, when laws are enacted but not enforced because some citizens are of the wrong color, or are not important enough to be heard or cared about, or they were born as women and not as men—the same ache of abandonment afflicts the human heart. Most talk about human rights tends to be rather empty until one sees for oneself the impact of these kinds of experiences. It is only then that we come to understand why certain rights are called *human* rights: because, quite simply, without them we are deprived of the full dignity of our human nature.

The blood that confirms the rule of law for the Hebrews serves as a divine guarantor that resources that make the full expression of life possible are protected and fostered by God. Those whose lives are directed by a spirituality of blood have a keen sense of how dependent we are on the patterns and rhythms that reinforce our basic humanity against the onslaught of disorder and the perversion of social and political oppression. Those patterns—be they simple day-to-day routines of human interaction or the constitutional aspects of a social pact—are part and parcel of what makes and keeps us human. Recovering alcoholics have to learn simple techniques that will keep them from falling back into their former habits. Parents who have lost a child in an accident must weave new patterns in their lives—patterns that do not depend upon the child's presence. And those who suffer the restrictions and arbitrariness of an unjust government have to struggle continually to reachieve some normalcy in their daily comings and goings. A spirituality of blood is a spirituality of the bonds that make and keep us human. It is a spirituality that attends especially to the fragility of all the patterns that reinforce us in our humanness—acts of acknowledgment and greeting, acts of simple hospitality, and political acts that protect and demand basic human rights.

A spirituality of blood, then, has to do with maintaining the good and proper ordering of society. As a symbol, blood holds within itself both death and life: a witness to the violence and disarray of shattered meanings and a celebration of humanity living in genuine peace. Those who share in this spirituality hold these realities always before them, living in solidarity with those who suffer, and living in hope for a better and more just world.

A Band of Slaves Turned into a People

The band of rebellious slaves wandering in the desert has been given a law, and has been constituted as a people. These marginated individuals, a no-people, once counted only as the chattel of others, now achieve a basic human dignity. They have their own identity and a God who cares for them in a special way.

On the south side of Chicago, an organization known as Operation PUSH (People United to Save Humanity) meets each Saturday morning in a former synagogue. Operation PUSH tries to help low-income blacks of the city toward a better life for themselves and their children. A familiar refrain that is part of the Saturday morning gathering is the shout "I am somebody!" The purpose is to help those who are told again and again, in any number of different ways, they count for nothing to realize that they are important—they are "somebody" not "nobody." For if individuals are not special to someone, if they do not belong somewhere, if they are never acknowledged, their lives begin to fragment and to dissipate. Children who have to enter a new school often suffer from being "nobodies" until they can reestablish themselves. Retirees, used to an active life, often discover that they are no longer needed or even noticed, and soon find themselves sinking into depression and premature death. Members of racial minority groups in a society will often feel like Ralph Ellison's *Invisible Man:* others treat them as though they simply were not there. If persons are subjected to this kind of treatment for too long, their personalities begin to disintegrate and they lose their sense of personhood.

The blood ritual in the Exodus story was about covenant. The blood traced a line around that motley band of slaves and made of them something special. And that blood became for the Hebrews more than the blood of young livestock; it became the blood that made of them a family, that gave them a shared substance of life and purpose—a shared substance that did not begin or end with any individual, but was part of a great stream carrying them from one generation to the next. It made them important to one another and to God.

A spirituality of blood attends especially to the bonding processes whereby individuals become somebodies rather than remaining nobodies. To be under the sign of blood is to reach out to persons who are caught in being nobodies and gather them into the circle of human warmth and affirmation. For that covenant bond has to be traced around them too, so that those who were on the outside become part of what is inside. The nobodies of the world, those pushed to the sidelines of society because they are too old, the wrong color, or disabled are called to inclusion, to a home, by those who follow a spirituality of blood. For just as the blood bond created the Hebrew people in the desert, so too the need for the recreation of human community continues into our own time.

The Blood Bond that Holds the World Together

If one concentrates on Moses' proclamation at the end of the Exodus story, all the different parts come together. "This is the blood of the covenant," he says. The blood becomes the bond that makes the covenant real and effective. And because of the blood bond, a new world has come about for the Hebrews.

The blood bond, the covenant, became the central way for Israel to speak of itself; its history becomes a history of covenants between God and the people. Whenever the relationship between God and Israel changes or needs to be restored, there is talk of covenant. And later in Israel's history, when Jesus tries to give expression to what God is bringing about through him, he turns to the language of covenant. It has been remarked that one of the meanings of the term "reign of God" is that of the restoration of God's covenant with the people (thus, God's reign, not the Romans' reign, over Israel). And before his death, Jesus speaks of the coming about of that reign as a "new covenant," this time sealed in his own blood (Lk. 22:19–20).

If there is a biblical image that is central to a spirituality of blood, it is certainly that of the covenant. For the symbol of blood, holding together within itself, as it does, the forces of life and death, becomes the medium for communication between God and Israel, expressing within itself the most fundamental messages about personhood and community, order and chaos, alienation and reconciliation, sin and forgiveness. The blood of the covenant speaks of the creation of human community through the bonding together of individuals, creating life in the wilderness of existence. It stands for somebodies where previously there were only nobodies.

Blood as a symbol bears within itself the sense of the costliness of the covenant and its fragility, and testifies to its incomparable power to forge life and hope in the death-dealing deserts of our time. Blood becomes the bond that holds the world together, built upon God's pledge to stay with us. "You will be my people and I will be your God": we are given a place to be, a home, when we seemed surrounded only by the endless desert with its predators. That covenant bond, sealed in blood, holds our world together.

·3

Life is in the Blood

*Since the life of every living body is in the blood, I have told the
Israelites: You shall not partake of the blood of any meat. (Lv. 17:14)*

The Book of Leviticus is not a favorite source for meditation on
the scriptures for most Christians. Yet if one is exploring the
biblical resources for a spirituality of blood, this book cannot
be ignored. Blood is referred to eighty-seven times there, more
than in any other book in the Bible.

To most readers, the Book of Leviticus seems to be an almost
endless list of prescriptions, relating to a world that seems very
distant from and even alien to our own. The references to defilement and cleansing, the offering of sacrifice, the detailed rules for
behavior and punishment of transgression all speak of a time and
place in which we cannot recognize ourselves.

Yet to understand much of the language of the New Testament,
and the whole framework for expressing the experience of salvation brought about in Jesus Christ, the language of Leviticus is
essential background. When the death of Christ is referred to as a
sacrifice for the sake of sin, when the Letter to the Hebrews talks of
Christ as the eternal high priest entering the sanctuary, or even
when the Letter to the Ephesians speaks of Christ as our peace, the
language and world of Leviticus is presumed.

So there is a need to examine something of this world in order to
make sense out of the later biblical witness. To ignore Leviticus is
to cut ourselves off from the resources of a great part of the New
Testament for Christian spirituality. Hence, there is little choice
but to plunge into this strange and often hard to comprehend
world.

But the interest here is more than technical. For if one moves a
little more deeply into what seems to be fairly alien or exotic

19

material, one begins to discover that the rites and prescriptions of Leviticus are responses to issues in human life still very much with us: undoing the damage of sin, dealing with the forces in our lives over which we have little or no control, giving shape and direction to our lives in the acknowledgment of our limitations and our finitude. When the rituals of Leviticus are viewed in this fashion, they start to make a little more sense. The language of sacrifice may be alien to most modern readers, but the needs it addresses are both ancient and new.

Five sets of rituals in Leviticus form background for the world of the New Testament and its discussion of what God has done for us in Jesus. By understanding a little better what motivated these rituals, we will be in a more favorable position to understand especially Paul's way of speaking of salvation. At the same time, a better understanding of these rituals can help clarify the dynamics addressed by a contemporary spirituality of the blood of Christ, and help make connections to our own time and place. The five rituals examined here are:

1. purificatory rites;
2. consecration rites;
3. sin offerings;
4. peace offerings;
5. expiatory rites.

Purificatory Rites

Menstruation, childbirth, the burial of the dead—all of these can make a person "unclean" or "impure." This seems quite strange to us today. Why would natural activities (menstruation and child-birth) and necessary activities (the burial of the dead) be considered unclean and lead to the isolation of those involved with them? In the case of menstruation and childbirth, it has been suggested (and with some justification) that these declarations of unclean-ness were yet another patriarchal ploy to keep women in subjugation. In the case of contact with a corpse, one might want to consider uncleanness as a way of talking about matters of contamination and hygiene. Yet the remedies for uncleanness—holocausts and sin offerings—hardly seem to have any medicinal value.

To understand why certain activities can make an individual

unclean, one has to step back a bit from the surface of these activities. Cleanliness and purity do not so much refer to physical contamination as they do to a different kind of defilement. What happens in menstruation and childbirth, as well as in dealing with the dead, is that individuals come into direct contact with the forces of life and death. In so doing, they go beyond the fragile boundaries of human society and community, into a zone where dwell powers far exceed the human capacity for endurance. The governing image here is one of human life as limited and frail, in need of care and protection. Human communities are surrounded by forces much greater than their own, forces with which they regularly need to come into contact, but forces that can easily overwhelm them. Perhaps a better word to describe contact with these forces than "unclean" or "impure" would be "dangerous."

When women conceive and bear children, it is not only dangerous for them physically, but they also touch in a more direct way than at any other point in human existence the mysterious forces of life. These forces are far greater than ours, forces with which we cannot bear long or continuous contact. The period of "uncleanness" is a social way of acknowledging that a woman bears within her forces that, left unchanneled, could overwhelm a society. Being set apart (or being in a period of "confinement") means that, although these contacts with dangerous powers are necessary for the survival of the community, they cannot become the normal way of things. The sacrifice that takes place at the end of the period of confinement is a way of reintegrating the woman into normal, day-to-day life. It is an acknowledgment that the period of danger is past, both for the woman and the society of which she is a member.

Likewise, physical contact with the dead is also a straying into the dangerous world beyond normal human existence. Those who touch the dead—who prepare the body for burial and carry out the burial itself—provide a necessary service to human society. Yet this unmediated contact with death introduces death into society in a direct way. These persons, too, are set apart and must be reintegrated back into normal, "safe" existence after their contact.

In both of these instances sacrifice—communicating with the realm of the divine where both the source of life and the dead dwell—is a bridge for crossing over into that world beyond and then safely returning. By crossing over and back, the boundary is confirmed. Sacrifice becomes a means of restoring normal patterns; it provides a bridge between our world and the world beyond, where God dwells. As was noted in the discussion of Exodus 24, for an ordinary human to cross into that world means certain death, with no chance of returning. Hence the ritual of sacrifice allows us, literally, to *do* the *sacred thing*. It allows us to communicate with God *and* return to our everyday existence.

Even with this explanation of why purificatory rites are prescribed, this whole world may still seem distant and alien to some readers. We need to take yet a further step. The guiding image here is that of the world as a hostile place, where human life and community are under continual threat. For those who live in comfortable and safe environments, and have access to a wide range of resources for dealing with threats to that environment (medicine, technology, sufficient wealth to allow for moving out of certain environments to other more favorable ones), this language of boundaries and danger zones makes little sense. That is perhaps why distinctions between pure and impure, clean and unclean, have largely disappeared in North American and European societies. They remain alive, however, in societal urgings to segregate and isolate things and events beyond control. Thus, fear of street crime will make some urban dwellers in Europe and North America want to segregate persons deemed alien and uncontrollable. This is seen in the reaction to Arab and Turkish workers in Swiss and German cities, or to blacks in U.S. cities. Fears about AIDS move some persons to call for isolation of its victims.

Those who live in hostile environments are more conscious of the need for establishing boundaries that allow them to be safe. Those who struggle to survive in harsh climatic zones have a strong sense of the boundaries that protect life. Those who must live in fear of roving death squads in parts of Central and South America know how important it is to be able to create zones of safety.

I would suggest that even below the layers of comfort and the sense of safety that persons experience in economies of abundance (as in Europe and North America), the older instincts of survival still press toward an image of the world divided into zones of safety and danger. Although medical technology has reduced the risks of childbirth to an extremely low level in those countries, ancient fears about life and death still haunt the scene. The resources of an economy of abundance speak against viewing the world in terms of constricting boundaries ("boundless opportunity" is the preferred image), but when persons in those cultures face situations they cannot control with their bounteous resources, they will find the old reflexes there. When no amount of medical technology stops the spread of cancer, when an accident robs someone of physical mobility, when a marriage shatters and cannot be put together again, we become acutely aware of how fragile and limited our lives are, and how much we need protection and care.

Purificatory rites have been a way of acknowledging this aspect of human existence. The prominence of the symbol of blood in the levitic sacrifices emphasizes how the forces of life and death are at work in each human situation. This is of course not to insist on purificatory rites in cultures where they make no sense; rather, it is to comprehend in some fashion what such rites are responding to: an acknowledgment of the fragility and limitations of all that we create in the name of our humanity, and the protection and care that such creations require.

A spirituality of blood, because it carries both life and death within its symbolism, creates a special awareness of this fragility of human constructions. Consequently, it evokes a sense of care and a sensitivity to the delicate nature of all that is human within us and around us. Although it need not urge a reversion to purificatory rites in cultures where these make no sense, it does recognize the human predicament addressed by those rites— namely, a need to acknowledge the limits that human existence comes up against when resources and efforts do not reach far enough. Those who live a spirituality of blood can dwell on those boundaries, accompanying others who suffer and want to do more, but cannot. By acknowledging the limits of human effort, they also affirm the strength and the beauty of what humans have been able to construct.

Consecration Rites (Lv. 8:14–30)

In this passage from Leviticus, Aaron and his sons are consecrated as priests for the people. This is accomplished with a sacrifice that atones for their sins and an anointing with the blood of the sacrificed animal. As a result of the consecration rites, Aaron and his sons take on special functions for the sake of the community at large.

Consecration has to do with making something holy or preparing something for a holy use. As with the purificatory rites, consecration rites, too, presume a certain view of the world. To consecrate something or someone is to set a thing or a person apart from ordinary use and activity. This setting apart carries with it a twofold message: (1) the instrument or person is no longer part of the ordinary aspect of human life; and (2) the presence of something or someone set apart locates the holy within the world. The fact that an instrument or person becomes restricted to action in certain areas attaches significance to those areas—they need special attention and care. The fact, too, that they are set apart reminds us how much the holy is not part of our world, that we inhabit a region much more diffuse in nature than the more densely textured world of the holy.

Consecration is a form of restriction, but it is at the same time a concentration or focusing of reality. Consecration acknowledges that the texture of human life is not uniform. Certain human relationships are more important to us than are others. Certain activities count more than do others. Rather than seeing life as an open plain, our accumulated experience tends to redraw the map of human life into points of greater density, which relate to one another as mountains relate to form a range. Consecration acknowledges that concentration or densification by a restriction that yields a focus. Just as it is important for persons, as they grow older, to have had a few possibilities well chosen and deeply explored rather than a limitless range of opportunities yet to be tested, so too by consecration individuals and societies find a means whereby they can express what is truly important to them, and acknowledge the limits of their existence. Consecration in the strict sense acknowledges the presence of the holy in the midst of the ordinary, and makes a dwelling place for it.

In the interests of reaffirming the goodness of creation, some religious persons make the point that, inasmuch as everything has been created by God, everything is holy. Therefore, the distinction between the holy and the ordinary is useless. Although there is truth in this, it seems to save one principle by giving up another. We humans have a hard time grasping totality, limited as we are. In a certain sense, to deem everything holy is to deem nothing holy. To return to an earlier observation: our lives do not admit of a uniform texture; rather they are punctuated by events by which we come to chart the rest of our experiences. Consecration need not imply that, because some things are set aside as holy, the rest of the environment is not. Instead, consecration is meant to help us negotiate the textured quality of our existence.

That blood played a central role in Israel's consecration rites is not surprising. As Leviticus reminds its readers on a number of occasions, blood is set apart for God because life itself is thought to reside in blood. Thus, the Israelites are not to partake of the blood. To use blood for anointing in a consecration rite, then, means that the altar, the vestments, and the person anointed now belong to God in a special way, and so can serve as mediators between God and the people.

In many pluralist societies in the West today, consecration would seem to be an outmoded way of relating to the world. The ideal is rather a role diffusion in the interests of achieving a more egalitarian society. Consecration would be seen as legitimating a stratification of classes in society. And that has indeed often been the case. But even professedly egalitarian societies will mask their forms of social stratification by not permitting acknowledgment of where patterns of differentiation actually lie. For example, employers in egalitarian societies are often expected to take on an easy informality with employees. But if an employee interprets that as genuine informality and starts to treat the employer as a peer and workmate, the employee may be in for a rude surprise when the employer reasserts power. Pretending that there is no difference may mask, therefore, where genuine differences are located.

The point of all this is that consecration helps identify, even in pluralist societies with egalitarian ideals, the texture of human relationships. In relating especially to the holy, the act of consecration provides a place for otherness to dwell in our midst, and offers us a window, as it were, upon that which transcends our existence.

Acts of consecration sometimes occur in our own day, not through prescribed ritual, but through witness in situations of conflict and violence. Such was the case with the murder of Father Stanley Rother in 1981 in the village of Santiago Atitlan in Guatemala. Rother had incurred the enmity of local officials for his championing the cause of the poor. Because of death threats, he had to change his sleeping place each night. On the morning of July 28, 1981, a death squad found him in the pantry of his little house and shot him there. That blood-spattered room has become a shrine for the local people, where they burn candles and leave flowers—a holy place anointed with the blood of a martyr.

A spirituality of blood is marked by an attentiveness to the sacrality that wells up in our midst. Although the forces of life and death are present together everywhere, they are especially concentrated in certain places: around pivotal events marking change in our lives, at moments of decision, at times when problems are resolved. At those moments, we have a view into a world much larger than our own. These are moments when the world of the holy comes into contact with our ordinary reality. Consecratory acts affirm and announce that we are indeed in a holy place, just as Jacob discovered after his dream (Gn. 28:16). We may not anoint those places with blood or oil, but in a spiritual sense we do mark them in memory. The Hebrews simply did it more concretely. A contemporary spirituality of blood tries to preserve that ability to recognize and celebrate the holy in our midst.

Sin Offerings (Lv. 4–5; 6:17–7:10)

A considerable amount of Leviticus is devoted to the sin offering. It should be noted at the outset that "sin" in this context does not mean only moral fault; it has to do with the transgression of any of the boundaries with the holy. Hence activities that would render someone unclean are also redressed by sin offerings. It was for that reason that any sacrifice could well begin with a sin offering, especially a sin offering for the priest performing the sacrifice.

The sin offering is meant to undo a transgression or sin. It is an undoing of history. It tries to get to the roots of wrongdoing and create the possibility of beginning over again. Without this prospect of overcoming sin and starting afresh, human life would simply sink away into the quagmire of its own finitude.

Sin offerings acknowledge that wrong has been done and needs to be righted. They also acknowledge that humans cannot of themselves straighten out what has been skewed. The profound nature of our relationship to God is not something to be taken lightly. When something goes wrong there, it cannot be quickly or easily set right. The consequences of human actions go much further than humans are able to reach. We do things that quickly get beyond our control, and we are incapable of undoing what has happened. A sharp word often cuts more deeply into another person than was intended, yet once done the damage is not easily erased. An act of betrayal, even when not intended, can destroy a marriage or a friendship. Put in another way, when we sin, we cannot give ourselves forgiveness; nor can we demand it of others.

Something has been initiated far larger than ourselves, something that can be dealt with only through the good agency of another.

In the sin offerings of Israel, the blood of the victim plays a central role. It is through the sprinkling of blood that the forgiveness of God is imparted. The blood is a sign that life has overcome the death-dealing acts of sin, that God has raised us above the depths to which we were sinking. Given the pervasive role of the sin offering in the temple cult—for individuals and for society as a whole—it is little wonder that it became a model for understanding the significance of Jesus' death for the early Christians. The blood of Christ the victim becomes the means whereby our alienation from God is overcome, whereby our sins are forgiven.

A spirituality of blood has to have as one of its dimensions a sense of the tragedy that the sin offering addresses. It recognizes how easily acts of life can slide into the realm of death, slipping out of the control of those who initiated them. Because the symbol of blood holds both life and death within it, it knows how quickly happy situations can be reversed, and how guilt and remorse, by themselves, are not redemptive. The sin offering of the Hebrews presented a concrete way of bringing about that redemption, and Christianity has developed its own sacramental ways of doing the same thing. Those who follow a spirituality of blood can walk with those who have known the anguish of sin and the relief of forgiveness. They are attuned to this tragic dimension of human existence and come to see in the saving blood of Christ a way out of the crushing dilemma of sin.

Peace Offerings (Lv. 3:1–17)

Peace offerings were sacrifices made in fulfillment of vows. The person providing the offering would also hold a sacred banquet at which the host and guests would feast upon the flesh of the sacrificial victim. Again, as in the other sacrifices, the blood was not consumed; it was splashed upon the altar as an offering to God.

Peace offerings were made by the nation in times of celebration, and by individuals as an act of thanksgiving for personal favors received. The symbolism of the banquet indicates the quality of the relationships between those making the offering and God, where all are around the same table, enjoying companionship and drawing their strength from the same food. This ritual, more than the others discussed here, emphasizes the communion aspect of sacrifice.

The peace offering also highlights in a special way the celebratory aspect of human life and community. It shows that important events need to be marked in a special way, and that the occasion calls for a reaffirmation of the bonding that makes human life and community possible. Of all the rituals under discussion here, the peace offering is the one perhaps least foreign to contemporary experience. Celebration is marked in almost every culture by festive eating and sharing.

As the descriptions of the various kinds of offerings indicate, the blood of the victim continues to figure prominently. Blood, as the source of our well-being, the gift of life, marks the sacrificial activity here once again. It provides the linkage between our world and the world of God.

There will be more opportunity later on to explore the celebratory meaning of a spirituality of blood, under the symbolism of the cup of blessing (chapter 6). However, for now it should be sufficient to note that such celebration is rooted in the fact that blood was seen as the origin of life. All that might develop by way of new possibilities, the fulfillment of dreams, the realization of expectations, springs up from that great source. So much of a spirituality of blood will be concerned with the brokenness of human existence and the care needed to attend to its fragile nature, but there is also a certain robust side to this spirituality as well, celebrating the great love that gives us the gift of life.

Expiation Rites (Lv. 16:1–34)

The Day of Atonement, as prescribed by the Book of Leviticus, was the most solemn day in the religious calendar. On that day, the high priest entered the Holy of Holies, bearing sacrificial blood. The sins of the people were expiated, and their iniquities were loaded upon a scapegoat, which was then driven into the wilderness. The day was marked by fasting, a sign of the nonordinariness of the occasion.

It was on this day that the sins of the people would be lifted from them and forgiven, giving them a chance for a fresh start. It was the time of the most intimate contact with God, as the high priest ventured into the very heart of the sanctuary, the only time of the year when this would happen. It marked in the most profound way the renewal of the covenant between God and Israel.

Ritual expiation, too, is hard for many of our contemporaries to understand. It strikes them as similar to the compulsive activity of the neurotic, an attempt to banish a anxiety through symbolic activity. In the atonement ritual, the goat takes away the sins of the people. Surely this is something that must be understood symbolically. For what do goats dying in the wilderness have to do with the forgiveness of human wrongdoing?

In its symbolic activity, ritual expiation gets at a deeper reality, going beyond the mere restitution with which many of our contemporaries would be more comfortable with as a response to sin. After all, restoring what has been lost would seem to be the most reasonable response to a sinful act. But ritual expiation aims at the deeper patterns of human life touched by sin, the dislocation in basic relationships, the skewing of trajectories in history. Ritual expiation tries to touch and undo not just the act itself, but the propensities that lead to sin, the roots in the human heart that feed sinful behavior. The annual atonement ritual of Israel is such an expiatory rite. It does not so much address specific sins as the firmly rooted sinfulness of a people.

A poignant contemporary example of expiation is the memorial to the victims of Dachau on the site of that former concentration camp. A large metal sculpture depicts victims struggling to escape the barbed wire surrounding the camp. One of the buildings that had housed inmates has been preserved, but the rest of the interior of the camp is an open, empty, silent space. A small museum documents in unblinking fashion the horrors perpetrated there, and shows a film of the camp's liberation in 1945. All of these things are meant to keep the camp in memory, lest forgetfulness pave the way to the same sin in the future.

At the north end of the camp is a chapel and convent of cloistered Carmelite nuns. The foundress of that convent decided to have it built there in the early 1960s, dedicating it to a constant vigil of prayer in expiation of the crimes committed at that place. She dedicated the chapel (which is open to the public; visitors can join the nuns in prayer) and the convent to the Precious Blood of Christ. In that setting it becomes painfully apparent what expiation through the blood of Christ means.

The sprinkling of the blood on the propitiatory in the Holy of Holies during the atonement ritual is the most direct contact with the divine reality that Israel was permitted. Israelites believed that God was more completely present above the propitiatory than anywhere else in the world. Blood, which belonged to God but was a gift to the living, was the medium for this contact.

It is not surprising, then, that the author of the Letter to the Hebrews uses the ritual of the Day of Atonement as a way of expressing what God has accomplished in the death of Jesus (Heb. 9). The most intimate and redemptive of contacts with God in Israel's experience becomes a way of talking about what Jesus has done on our behalf. The language and imagery of the Letter to the Hebrews depends heavily upon this sacrificial imagery. And as long as humans engage in crime and sin, there will be a need to reach beyond restitution into the patterns of ritual expiation.

Conclusion

Special ritual activity seems to be necessary when we find ourselves beyond a realm we can control. All too often we come up against the limits of our efforts and achievements, or we find ourselves needing to undo what we have done. Symbolic activity tries to give voice to the things we cannot say, to encompass experiences we cannot fully grasp.

The ritual activity that the Hebrews developed for those situations all involved the use of blood, for blood carried within its symbolism the same ambiguity about life and death, about potential and limit, that those situations exhibited. By means of blood, as a substance sacred to God, breaches in the life of the community could be bridged and the world could be restored to integrity.

Blood rituals of this type are no longer practiced in most of the world's cultures today, but there is something about them that has endured. As long as human life deals with finitude and sinfulness, and as long as it yearns for a wholeness that transcends finitude and brokenness, it must find a way to symbolize its redemption. A spirituality of the blood of Christ has this kind of awareness at its center. It is not only a celebration of life, nor is it only a brooding on the forms of death that stalk a limited and often fractured world. It has to do with redemption, an overcoming of obstacles. It has to do with liberation from the bondage of finitude. It has to do with nourishing the dreams of hope that keep the human heart alive.

Treading the Winepress

Who is this that comes from Edom,
  in crimsoned garments, from Bozrah—
This one arrayed in majesty,
  marching in the greatness of his strength?
"It is I, I who announce vindication,
  I who am mighty to save."
Why is your apparel red,
  and your garments like those of the wine presser?
"The winepress I have trodden alone,
  and of my people there was no one with me.
I trod them in my anger,
  and trampled them down in my wrath;
Their blood spurted on my garments;
  all my apparel I stained.
For the day of vengeance was in my heart,
  my year for redeeming was at hand." (Is. 63:1–4)

This haunting poem, with its vivid imagery of a lone warrior returning from battle, his clothing soaked in blood, is a remarkable piece of literature, and presents one of the most unusual images of God that we find in all the scriptures. For the lonely warrior in the blood-soaked clothing, who answers the watchman's questions, is none other than Jahweh. Christian tradition has at times identified this strange figure also with Jesus in his passion, treading in solitude the winepress of sin. One finds Jesus so represented in the art of both East and West. Those familiar with traditional Roman Catholic spirituality of blood will recall also Max Walz's little book, *Why Is Thy Apparel Red?*, published in 1914, which developed this connection with Jesus in a special way.

But if one reads the Isaian text more closely, one is likely to draw back from such a quick identification of the warrior with Jesus.

The solitude of the figure in the winepress is certainly reminiscent of Jesus facing his destiny alone, but the warrior does not seem to be a suffering victim. On the contrary, he is portrayed as "marching in the greatness of his strength." And he is shown as fiercely angry—hardly the silent, submissive figure of Calvary. When one reflects on this just a bit more it becomes unmistakably apparent that what we have here before us is the image of an angry, avenging God, crushing the bodies of enemies in an all-consuming wrath. A few verses further on in the same poem, this image of a ferocious God is all too evident:

> I trampled down the peoples in my anger,
> I crushed them in my wrath,
> and I let their blood run out upon the ground.
> (Is. 63:6)

This does not sound like the God who creates a special people in the desert, or who is known for protecting the weak. Or does it?

What contributions does this remarkable poem make to a spirituality of blood? As we have seen, it has long been associated with such a spirituality, albeit through a kind of christological transposition, applying it to the suffering Christ rather than to a warrior God. In order to clear our minds a bit from a more familiar interpretation of the passage, it might be useful first to look at what this poem was trying to convey in its own context as a way for us to approach it in a new fashion.

Background to the Text

This poem forms part of what some exegetes have called the "apocalypse" at the end of the Book of Isaiah. In the last ten chapters of Isaiah, a recurrent theme is the coming of a savior and the end of the present age. The six verses of this short poem are inserted in the middle of the Isaian oracles. They contain some unusual vocabulary, as well as some of the most striking images of the entire scriptures.

The poem is cast as a dialogue. A watchman on the ramparts of Jerusalem sees a figure approaching. That figure strides along, coming from the direction of Bozrah, one of the major cities of Edom. At the time of Isaiah, the Edomites were being pushed out of their own country by the Nabataeans. Having no place else to go, they turned west, and were running raids on Judah. At this time, the Edomites were seen as a threat and potential enemy to the kingdom of Judah.

When asked to identify himself, the approaching figure identifies himself simply as God, by giving no other name than the first-person pronoun—the same "I" who spoke the word of salvation to Moses from out of the burning bush (Ex. 3:14). And in this situation, too, the warrior-God speaks of vindication and salvation for the people. In asking the warrior about the color of his garments, the watchman makes the suggestion that the warrior may have been in the winepress, for his garments have the red stains of someone who has been pressing grapes. Edom, after all, was famous for its wine, and in Hebrew "Edom" and "red" share the same root *(dm)*.

But the warrior does not allow any such innocent associations between the making of wine and the color of his garments. The red in his garments comes not from the blood of grapes (as wine was sometimes called), but from the blood of his enemies, whom he has crushed beneath his might as grapes in a winepress. God has avenged the enemies of Judah by ruthlessly crushing them under foot. Vengeance, the warrior says, was in my heart. The deed seems to have been performed in a fierce anger against the enemies of the people.

And this act of vengeance is carried out by God alone, without any help from the people of Judah. What is striking, too, is that no one from Judah actually witnesses God's act; nor does anyone bring back advance word of the avenging battle. Only God, the lone warrior, reports its occurrence.

The Blood of Wrath

In the reflections on the meaning of blood in the Book of Exodus, the life-giving power of the blood received the greater emphasis. The blood in the Passover account protected the Hebrews from death, and the blood at Sinai made them into a new people, cared for in a special way by God. Even the accounts of blood sacrifices in the Book of Leviticus were about restoring life after sin and ritual uncleanness. In those stories blood always reflects Israel's protection by God and the covenant bond of commitment between God and the people.

But if one surveys the entire Hebrew scriptures, one will discover that, even though Israel associates blood with life, with its ability to purify, blood is more often used in the context of death and destruction. Blood that is poured out becomes a mark of violence, of death, of chaos. All the somber images of anger, vengeance, and violence start to tumble out upon us as this side of the symbol is opened up: images of violent irruptions of uncontrollable rage, of the unleashing of long-harbored resentments, in which the angers of another time are now played out upon the heads of innocent victims. Images of dissolution into chaos and death emerge as blood spurts out from the pierced and shattered body. Deep trauma, and then an awful stillness. The deep fears of the human psyche are brought to the surface when we are confronted with this dreadful violence.

It cannot be forgotten that the symbolism of blood has to do with all these things too, not just with the warmth of community and the ruddy glow of life. The symbolism of blood, both in the scriptures and in human society, gains as much of its power to convey experience from this ominous, negative side as it does from the more positive dimension. It is precisely this that has made blood such a powerful symbol for expressing the dilemmas of human existence, because it does hold together both life and death within itself.

We know that the symbolism of blood does indeed carry within it all these things, but what place does this negative side have in a contemporary spirituality of blood? Does the image of the winepress, with blood spurting out as human bodies are crushed, have anything positive to offer us?

There are some things, I believe, that deserve our exploration. The first of these is the connection between blood and wrath. If we are to understand discussion about the redemptive suffering of Jesus, we need to appreciate the relationship between blood and wrath.

In efforts to build up the life of a community, and to bring together a plurality of hopes and dreams into something of a shared vision, anger is usually seen as something destructive of this process, and therefore something to be avoided. Anger seems to tear up the fragile bondings that create a sense of community and belonging. It always threatens to go further than intended, wrecking more than its immediate objective. It always carries with it an undertone of rejection, a rejection that threatens to undo all the hard work of community-building that has gone on.

But anger can arise out of a perception of injustice. An individual or group feels profoundly wronged in a situation, and therefore reacts in anger. Those perceptions may not always be correct: they may arise out of selfishness on the part of the individual or group, or from misperceptions of the intentions of others. But one cannot assume immediately that anger is wrongheaded. Sometimes the perceptions of injustice that vent themselves in anger are rooted in reality. And when injustice comes to be ingrained in a community or a society over a period of time and starts to attack the very possibility of decent relationships among its members, then anger grows into a mighty wrath.

And that sorry situation is in evidence in too many places: persons growing up in circumstances where first their parents, and later their employers and spouses, put them down and demean them; situations where it is taken for granted that persons will not have enough to eat, will not receive an education, and will not have much chance of decent employment; societies where citizens may be deprived of their liberty or even their lives at the whim of a government official. Such situations are not uncommon. And in all of them wrath continues to accumulate.

This wrath is a protest, a protest against allowing the forces of death to dictate how life must be lived. Most often the wrath cannot go beyond protest: it does not have the resources to overcome injustice. Hence a great fund of wrath may continue to accumulate in an individual's heart as mistreatment continues at every turn; a people constrained in its liberties will harbor a wrath that expresses itself from time to time in demonstrations against its oppressor. The denial of basic human needs will create a protest looking for an outlet that may help liberate a people from its repression. The deep frustration encased in such wrath stems from the realization that it probably cannot overcome the injustice it endures. It receives temporary outlet in protest, but in fact continues to accumulate and create a growing pressure like some underground volcano, which at some unforeseen moment will erupt and release its awesome energies in many directions at once.

In this passage from Isaiah and in many others within the scriptures, God is pictured as being filled with wrath. The wrath is provoked by the injustice wreaked upon the powerless, the weak, and the poor. That blazing wrath then scorches the earth when it erupts, and wipes out evildoers. In this passage from Isaiah, which is one of the most graphic portrayals of God's wrath, God sets out to crush the opponents of the people of Judah, God's special people. God's wrath brings about a vindication that our wrath cannot.

But what is the connection here between blood and wrath? The sign of blood evokes the memory of wrath and of injustice. When persons are alive and well, we do not see blood. It is only when they have been pierced and their bodies shattered that blood is in evidence. To see blood is to know that something is wrong. Every time that blood is seen or is brought to awareness, the memory of the wrongs, the injustices, and the continuing patterns of oppression in our world stand once again before us. Anger at all the sin, the wrongs, and injustices still unreconciled in our hearts and in our society blazes up before us. We are very much aware that the good often suffer in our world, and sometimes suffer precisely because they are good. And this awareness does not make living with those realities any easier. The wrath that blazes out is a sign that justice has not yet been done.

Blood keeps before us the memory of the suffering of the innocent, the wronged, and the defenseless. Its staining power does not permit us to overlook the harsh and wrongful circumstances under which we live—the circumstances that make such suffering possible. It reminds us how deeply suffering runs in our society, and how firmly rooted are the injustices against which we struggle.

Memory is an essential aspect of who we are as individuals and as a people. To allow certain memories to glide away into oblivion is sometimes a way of reassuring ourselves that they did not happen or do not really matter. The Nobel Peace Prize winner Elie Wiesel has made a lifelong calling out of keeping the memory of the Jewish Holocaust before the consciousness of the West. As he has said on numerous occasions, there are too many who want to forget this horrible event that scars the face of Western civilization. By letting it disappear from our awareness, we say in effect that it is really not worth remembering. And so Wiesel continues to speak and to write in order to keep that memory alive.

One aspect of a spirituality of blood is a cultivation of memory. Wrongs that have been reconciled and forgiven might well move beyond memory as the healing of hearts takes place, but memories that still roil with wrath against injustice must be kept before us so that someday a healing may take place. For if the frame of memory is removed from the anger that results from injustice, wrath turns into rage. Wrath is anger directed at the source of injustice, but rage has no such sharply focused object. Rage is wrath that has lost its focus and in its destructive sweep may bring about new pain and injustice. The clearest example, too often repeated in human history, occurs when wrath is either so frustrated or so immense that it turns from protest to rioting. A riot is unfocused rage. When individuals or groups go on a rampage, destroying whatever stands in their path (memories of enraged and disenfranchised farmers in the American Midwest come to mind, or the riots in South African townships), it says in effect that justice is no longer possible, that reconciliation is now beyond the pale of possibility.

When wrath turns into rage, it is not simply an oppressor who is the object of its destructive power. When wrath turns into rage, the anger can also crush those who are oppressed. It may seem to be cathartic, but it leaves the situation basically unchanged.

Blood, then, is part of the frame of memory that keeps open a channel for vindication. The Christian eucharist, with its ritual of holding up and sharing the cup of the blood of Christ, is part of a strategy to continue to struggle for justice in this way. As the German theologian Johannes Metz has pointed out, the memory of what happened to Jesus is a "dangerous memory" in the history of suffering. Jesus, the sinless one, is executed as a public criminal, on charges that demonstrate at least some misconception of what his ministry and message were all about. That God has vindicated Jesus' death by raising him from the dead becomes a sign and guarantee that the sufferings of the followers of Jesus in the present age, both those lodged in individual histories of pain and in communal memories of oppression, will one day experience God's own vindication as well. The holding up and sharing of the cup of Christ's blood both recalls and reinforces the memory of what God has done for Jesus and will do for those who suffer today.

So the sign of blood can offer more than a memory of wrath. It is more than an awareness of injustices still to be righted. One of the basic meanings of blood in this context is that there is a way through wrath to vindication and reconciliation. One does not deal with wrath by denying its existence, especially when wrath continues to be fed by injustice. This is often the fault of those who call too readily for reconciliation, because they have not felt the crushing pain of injustice in their own bodies. Those who are oppressed cannot forget vindication; it is the necessary prelude to any reconciliation, for vindication is an acknowledgment of how deeply the furrow of pain has cut through the human heart of the sufferer. In radio broadcasts from black churches in the United States on a Sunday morning, the death of members of the congregation is often spoken of in terms of vindication, for awareness of racism is a constant in the black community. Only death, only being gathered to the bosom of Abraham, can provide relief from that oppression. Now home with God, those who have died are free at last.

In this poem from Isaiah, wrath is overcome by the vindicating warrior-God. In the New Testament, the theme of wrath and vindication is taken up in the redemptive suffering of Christ, whose blood is a sign of God's overcoming the evil of the present age. This theme, which has been central to the message of Christian salvation, will be explored in more detail a little later on, below. It is in the sufferings of Christ that Christians believe that sin and injustice will eventually be overcome.

The Winepress

In the poem, the warrior picks up on the allusion to wine-making that the watchman had suggested. The warrior describes his vindication as a crushing of the bodies of his enemies, as one would crush grapes. This image appears elsewhere in the scriptures, notably in the Book of Revelation (14:18–20), where the harvest of souls is placed in the winepress of God's wrath.

In Christian tradition, the image of the winepress appears frequently as part of a spirituality of blood, for wine was known in Semitic culture as "the blood of grapes." This image was particularly popular in medieval iconography, where either Christ treads the winepress or is himself crushed in it. Christ's being crushed in the winepress brings us somewhat closer to the Revelation use of the image, where both the good and the bad are thrown into the press and crushed.

The images of the winepress in Isaiah 63 and Revelation 14 offer two distinctive contributions to a spirituality of blood. In the Isaian use of the image, God brings justice to the people by crushing its enemies. The winepress represents a kind of crucible of human society, a place where all the conflicts and injustices in society come to be concentrated. Here those conflicts and injustices are crushed, but crushed by God and God alone.

One of the important aspects of a spirituality of blood, as alluded to above in the discussion on blood and wrath, is to find a way through suffering and injustice to vindication and healing. One of the ways of doing so is through our solidarity in Christian commitment and ministry with those who suffer and those who seek justice. This idea of solidarity finds its roots in the covenant, a theme explored above. The blood of the covenant seals in its solidarity not only those who are already redeemed, but also those still questing for justice.

Important as solidarity is, and as crucial as being able to walk with those who suffer continues to be, the passage from Isaiah 63 reveals to us also that there are some injustices that our solidarity cannot overcome, our struggles for justice cannot supercede. Some injustices remain to be dealt with by God alone. That is why God alone treads the winepress, and why a point is made of it in this poem. There are injustices that God alone can redress, injustices that only God can vindicate for those who suffer. When that vindication will take place is not at all clear. In the poem, the vindication comes as a surprise to the watchman, who is alert and the first in Jerusalem to know of it, but nonetheless is surprised by the event. The element of surprise suggests that such vindication takes place when God decides, not when we decide. A hint, however, is given in verse 4: "my year for redeeming is at hand." Exegetes see this as a reference to the jubilee year, when all debts are remitted and the community of Israel can begin afresh. In view of God's declaration of a jubilee year, some distant, eschatological vindication need not be the only possibility for redressing the wrongs of the age. Perhaps a jubilee year will soon be upon us.

All of this is not to suggest giving up the struggle for justice, nor is it an excuse for lapsing into passivity. The image of the winepress suggests that there are certain injustices, on an almost cosmic level, that cannot conceivably be resolved without divine intervention. To know when to struggle and when to wait upon the Lord is the sign of a certain spiritual maturity. When one looks to the life of Jesus, and especially to his suffering and death, one sees this dialectic at work. On the one hand, Jesus quite deliberately sets his sights on Jerusalem in order to preach the message of God's impending reign. On the other hand, the accounts of the Last Supper and his prayerful struggle in the garden after the meal reflect Jesus' own wrestling with the need both to assert the message of God given to him and to leave the final inbreaking of that reign in God's hands. His own way of the cross and death recount his having turned over the struggle to God.

The image of blood reminds us not to give up the struggle, not let the frame of memory be broken. But each sighting of blood reminds us, too, that blood will continue to be shed, that ultimate vindication is still not at hand. Besides a sign of memory, the blood becomes a sign of waiting, and with it, a sign of hope.

Revelation 14:18–20 offers a second perspective on a spirituality of blood. In this passage, the winepress serves as the crucible of living and suffering into which all human beings, good and bad, just and unjust, are gathered. All are crushed under God's wrath. The blood of all of them flows out of the press. Commentators have seen in this passage a response to the question of why the just suffer, of why the innocent undergo pain. Here all are mixed together, and all feel God's wrath. Even those who seem innocent and just are in some way deserving of God's wrath against sin and injustice, but the measure of God's requital seems unfair. The innocent and the just suffer at least as much as do evildoers, if not even more, precisely because they are so much less deserving of affliction.

As a way of responding to this problem, a traditional interpretation has been that suffering is a pathway through which God leads the innocent and the just in order to purify them completely and to elevate them to a new and more intimate relationship with the divine reality. The paradigmatic example for this is, of course, Jesus: he who knew no sin was made sin for us (2 Co. 5:21).

Attempts to interpret this suffering of the innocent are, at bottom, admissions that we simply do not know why the innocent must suffer. However, we do know that suffering is not always destructive of these persons; sometimes it brings them to a more refined spiritual level and makes them guides for the rest of us in our own afflictions. If Jesus is the central revelation of God in our history, and Jesus as an innocent victim suffered unjust death, then that paradox of innocent suffering and ultimate vindication must lie somehow at the center of our world and our understanding of God. The interpretation of innocent suffering as purifying is an attempt to give expression to this paradox. It may not be the best interpretation, and a purifying elevation does not always occur (one sees this especially in the suffering of children not old enough to understand what is happening to them). Yet it does provide one way to begin to address a vexing problem at the heart of human existence.

The blood flowing from this winepress is mingled blood: the blood of the innocent and the blood of wrongdoers. Because it is mingled, it can no longer be distinguished. The symbols are muddled together.

A spirituality of blood is not a "tidy" spirituality, because the appearance of blood is not something tidy. Those who might seek a more ordered and neatly arranged way of life will not be attracted to this as a central symbol to orient their response to the gospel. Besides the alienating experience that the shedding of blood provokes in us, blood stains what it touches, leaving its mark long after its first appearance. To live a spirituality of blood is to live with considerable ambiguity. The activities that led Jesus to the shedding of his blood were at the time by no means clear except about their outcome: they would surely lead to his death. In that way, the winepress of Revelation is an apt symbol for this spirituality, because it captures the ambiguity of the wheat and the weeds growing together until harvest time, when the great judge will sort all things out.

We all know persons who have felt the heavy tread of the winepress upon them. These two interpretations of the winepress might help them comprehend or somehow explain their own situation. Perhaps the oppressive heel they now feel on their bodies can be lifted only by God. They may know that they are remembered by the believing community in their suffering, but when they are imprisoned, battered, and pierced, it seems to them that there is no rescue in sight. Only the one who is mighty to save (Is. 63:1) shall indeed one day bring vindication.

The image from Revelation may be more appropriate: to see the present time, especially in the case of an injustice that we cannot overcome, as a time of purification, of preparation for a better age when new and solid virtue will be needed to stop the wheel of injustice from turning. Those who have been tried in adversity will lead the struggle to bring injustice to a halt.

At any event, the image of blood, prominent in both Isaiah and Revelation, keeps us from spiritualizing away the harsh realities of the present situation. Suffering experienced now is no less real or less painful just because it will someday be avenged. And blood does not allow us to forget that. What these interpretations do provide is a support for the hope dwelling within us, the hope that helps us stay faithful to a God who promises vindication and justice.

Garments Crimson and Blood-stained

A final contribution from this passage to a spirituality of blood comes in the reference to the garments of the warrior. The garments are both crimson (the color of royalty) and blood-stained from battle. This combination of purple and red was another reason why the Isaian warrior came to be identified with Christ, who was both Lord and crucified victim.

What is important here is the combination. From a distance, the watchman sees only the crimson of the warrior's garments. Closer up, the blood stains become evident. From a distance we tend to see God as the all-powerful, the God beyond conflict. Close up, however, we see a God much closer to our reality—still deeply wrathful because of the injustices perpetrated upon the lowly of this world, but immersed in our reality as concretely as the blood that stains the warrior's garments. God is not beyond our conflicts, but struggling with us in the very midst of them.

Those who are followers of Jesus will show the marks of blood upon their garments as well. Although we do not *enjoy* conflict, much of the reality we must confront is of a conflictual nature. A spirituality of commitment and ministry must acknowledge the presence of conflict—sometimes direct out-and-out confrontation, sometimes conflict that is repressed and hidden. Those who follow Jesus will become blood-stained; but that is the only way that the crimson garment will come to us. The white robes of the saints in the Book of Revelation have been washed in the blood of the Lamb (Rv. 7:14). To find our way to the throne of God, we must pass with that God through the sufferings of the present time.

Conclusion

This passage from Isaiah has permitted us to explore another side of the symbolism of blood as it appears in the scriptures. It is less comforting, less inspiring, perhaps, than the symbolism of the blood of the covenant. But without exploring the blood of wrath and the winepress, we will not be able to understand the redemptive value of the shedding of Christ's blood. Suffering and the enduring of violence are not of themselves redemptive. Indeed, it almost always takes some power from outside the given situation to make them redemptive. Likewise, not to contemplate blood in this dimension is to deprive ourselves of an important resource for a spirituality of conflict. For it is in conflict that the imagery of blood receives a special concreteness, and Christians receive the concrete call to solidarity with the poor and those who suffer, to enter into the heart of conflict.

That call is discomforting to the comfortable, but it is the voice of hope to those who suffer, to those who grow tired with the grinding weight of chronic physical pain, of struggling with racial oppression and never-ending poverty, and to those who must wait through the long nights of their loss. Like the blood on the doorposts of the Hebrew slaves in Egypt, this blood, too, is a sign: not a sign of protection or liberation, perhaps; but a sign of memory and hope.

·5

The Prayer that Leads to Blood

In his anguish [agony] *he prayed with all the greater intensity, and his
sweat became like drops of blood falling to the ground. (Lk. 22:44)*

The biblical texts considered thus far have been foundational
for understanding the way the early church came to interpret
the meaning of Christ's suffering and death as redemptive in
the light of Israel's history. In the texts from Exodus, Leviticus, and
Isaiah, we find an interweaving of themes that came to give a more
concrete and sculptured character to the symbolism of blood as
the basis for a spirituality: themes of protection; of life and death;
of covenant and law; of experiencing limitation and seeking forgiveness; of wrath, vindication, and justice. These themes com-
posed the backdrop against which the life and death of Jesus came
to be understood by the early church.

With the New Testament texts, my concern will be to center the
spirituality of blood more directly on the blood of Christ. For it is
in a following of Christ that any Christian spirituality must find its
foundation.

The first of the New Testament texts to be considered comes from
the Gospel of Luke. The pericope is embedded in a narrative about
Jesus' prayer on the Mount of Olives immediately prior to his
arrest. There are parallel accounts in the Gospels of Matthew
(26:36–46) and Mark (14:32–42). The story is generally known
among Christians as the "agony in the garden." For those familiar
with traditional devotions to the blood of Christ, this story is the
basis for the second of the traditional seven bloodsheddings of
Christ. It also constituted the first of the sorrowful mysteries of the
fifteen-decade rosary.

The story has always held a special appeal for Christians, because Jesus is portrayed here with very human characteristics. As

44

in the story of Lazarus, where Jesus weeps for his dead friend, Jesus is seen here as someone struggling with the meaning of his life and the consequences of his decisions. He sees before him the prospect of arrest and death, and he struggles to come to grips with it. He looks for support from his disciples, but finds none. After intense prayer, Jesus accedes to what he understands as God's will for him.

In published meditations on this episode in Jesus' life, especially those connected with devotion to the blood of Christ, the points highlighted in this story are the intensity of Jesus' love for us and Jesus' obedience to God. The drops of blood falling to the ground underline the intensity of the situation for Jesus, how much love and obedience are costing him both physically and spiritually. All these motifs can be found in the combined accounts of Matthew, Mark, and Luke. The sheer humanity of Jesus portrayed in these texts shows us both someone with whom we can identify, and a model for living our own lives.

But this interpretation, time-honored though it is, depends to some extent on a conflation of the three Gospel accounts. It chooses elements from each and then in effect creates a story that does not correspond exactly to any one of the three original accounts. It would be useful to sort out those three accounts from their popular conflation. By attending especially to Luke, and then comparing it with the accounts given by Matthew and Mark another motif emerges, one that contributes in a distinctive way to a spirituality of the blood of Christ. We need to begin, then, by looking closely at the text in Luke.

The Lukan Narrative (Lk. 22:39–46)

Matthew and Mark's versions of this story show a high degree of parallelism; Luke's rendition stands apart. Matthew and Mark say that Jesus went to pray in a place called Gethsemane. Luke says that Jesus went to the Mount of Olives to pray, "as was his custom" (22:39). Jesus is more anxious and restless in the Matthean and Markan accounts: he goes to pray three times, and three times comes back to check on the disciples. This going back and forth heightens the sense of drama in the story. Jesus' prayer is intense, but he is also clearly distracted by the absence of support from the disciples. In the Lukan narrative, Jesus leaves the disciples and goes off to pray, returning only when he has finished. Only Luke's version has a reference to Jesus' being in agony, to his sweat becoming like drops of blood, and to the angel strengthening him.

A common interpretation of this story depicts Jesus as struggling with his decision, seeking the disciples' support and not getting it, returning to pray twice, and then praying so intensely the third time that his sweat becomes like drops of blood. An angel comes to give him the support he cannot get from his disciples.

Thus the rather uncertain and struggling Jesus of Matthew and Mark is put together with the more serene Jesus of Luke, who is strengthened by an angel and sweats blood. The result gives an image of a Jesus struggling with his destiny to the point of entering an acute psychological state. If this is correct, it prompts a question: Why do Matthew and Mark not include the bloodshedding in their story, for it would have enhanced the sense of drama they were apparently trying to create? And conversely: Why does Luke include the angel and the bloodshedding when the rest of his narrative is so subdued—Jesus going to his regular place to pray and not seeming overconcerned about receiving support from his disciples?

The Story: Preparation for the Ultimate Contest

It has been suggested that the key to this riddle might lie in Luke's introduction of the word *agonia* into the narrative. In the subsequent tradition, because of the use of that word in this narrative, *agonia* has come to mean acute psychological suffering, especially in connection with a decision that has to be made. Thus, I might say that making a certain decision was agonizing for me. We also talk about agony in terms of physical suffering, especially in the case of the final struggle before death.

Agonia has to do with struggle, to be sure. But its general meaning at the time of Jesus was struggle in an athletic contest. It referred especially to the mental preparation an athlete would undergo before entering the arena. That mental preparation was paired with physical exercises to prepare the muscles of the body for the exertion of the contest. In American slang, *agonia* might be translated "psyching up."

If we follow out this interpretation of the word in the context of Luke's narrative, we have Jesus going to his accustomed place of prayer to prepare himself for the final combat with the forces of evil. The angel appears to strengthen him, much as the athletic trainer would monitor the mental and physical preparation of the athlete. An angel appears as the trainer because this is no ordinary athletic combat; it is a duel with the forces of evil. Jesus then continues his preparation and moves into a final stage during which his prayer, his communion with God, becomes so intense that his sweat becomes like drops of blood. The sweat, then, is not an indication of anxiety; it is the result of the physical and mental exertion Jesus is undergoing.

How does Jesus himself characterize what he is doing on the Mount of Olives? In both verses 40 and 46 he urges his disciples to pray that they might not be subjected to "the test." It seems that Jesus assumes *he* will be so subjected, but there is a chance that they might escape.

And what is this test? It is not a test in the sense of a temptation, as it has sometimes been interpreted. It is a test of strength or of endurance in a battle with the powers of evil. Jesus alludes to this when he says to those who have come out to arrest him, "But this is your hour—the triumph of darkness!" (v. 53). Jesus, then, is preparing himself on the Mount of Olives for the supreme contest of his mission. It is now no longer a matter of struggling with an individual demon or a group of demons, as he does elsewhere in the Gospel of Luke. It has now become a matter of taking on the combined forces of evil. There is a reference to this same ultimate contest in Luke 12:49–50: "I have come to light a fire on the earth. How I wish the blaze were ignited! I have a baptism to receive. What anguish I feel till it is over!"

And how does Jesus fare in the contest? Luke presents Jesus as performing remarkably well. He never loses his self-composure, either with those arresting him, or with those who conduct the hearings against him. He remains calm on the way to the cross, admonishing the weeping women to weep rather for themselves and their children, and not for him (23:28). He forgives his executioners (23:34) and welcomes the good thief into paradise (23:43). And finally he himself dies, commending his spirit to God (23:46). He is a well-seasoned athlete, achieving victory. He has defeated the powers of evil in the contest.

Luke's version of the story can be read as Jesus' undertaking his passion and death as an athlete undertakes a contest, a contest that probes his resolve and virtue. The "agony" on the Mount of Olives was that of an athlete preparing for a contest.

The athletic metaphor appears elsewhere in early Christianity, notably in the Pauline literature (e.g., 1 Co. 9:24–27; 2 Tm. 4:7–8), and in the passion accounts of the early martyrs. To run the race, to fight the good fight, was a way of talking about the struggle to be faithful to God. It called for single-mindedness, discipline, and strength for endurance. To withstand sin, temptation, and evil was to win the prize, the imperishable crown, to achieve ultimate victory. The fact that some martyrdoms took place in arenas led to their being recounted as athletic contests—between Christians and their executioners. A Christian death, in which allegiance to Jesus had not been abjured, was taken as a victory, with Christ himself rewarding the crown.

But what of the bloodshedding as part of Jesus' preparation? Luke is careful to frame this within the context of the *agonia*, the preparation for struggle. In that agony, "he prayed with all the greater intensity, and his sweat became as drops of blood falling to the ground."

In the athletic manuals of the time, trainers distinguished different kinds of sweat, marking different stages of athletic preparation and competition. The sweat would be different, depending upon the interaction of the humors of the body. In those manuals, instances were cited of concentration so intense that drops of blood appeared. This was considered the highest form of concentration. Such sweating of blood has been known to happen. Explained according to modern Western medicine, neural activity over-stresses certain small capillaries under the surface of the skin, rupturing them, and blood escapes with moisture in the perspiration process. This can happen under heightened neural activity and situations of acute stress. In Jesus' case, then, the stress was not breaking him down; rather, like a good athlete, he was reaching the peak of his powers, ready to go into contest against the demons and powers of evil.

Seeing Jesus' agony in this way also explains why the angel comes to strengthen him before he sweats drops of blood, rather than to comfort him after he does so. The angel is the athletic trainer, helping him in the final stage of preparation.

A Spirituality of Struggle and Situations of Conflict

Why this emphasis on a different reading of the story from Luke? Often we can become so used to reading a text in a certain way that we neglect parts of it that do not fit our perception. Luke makes something considerably different of this prelude to the passion—different from the treatment by Matthew and Mark. The traditional image we have of the garden scene is really derived from Matthew and Mark. And it is a fair reading of those texts. But what has happened in the Christian imagination is that two dramatic elements from Luke's account—the appearance of the angel and the sweating of blood—have been conflated into the Matthean-Markan account of the story. Those elements are then interpreted as emphasizing Matthew and Mark's message.

But to leave the story at only that interpretation is to deprive ourselves of some of the great resources the scriptures offer us. Luke's account, taken in its integrity, yields a slightly different version, and a different spirituality of the blood of Christ as well.

The Matthean-Markan reading underscores the suffering that Jesus underwent in trying to conform his will to the will of his Father. He hesitates, he seeks the help of his disciples, but then finds himself alone before the decision. Yet he ends in obedience to his Father's will. As a result of this, we have in Jesus an example of one who understands the anguish we have to go through in discerning and then accepting what God sees for us as our own mission in life. We can count on the comfort of Jesus to help us, for that is guaranteed by Jesus' own experience and the shedding of his blood. Blood here means that there is no mental anguish that Jesus has not known, and no anguish of ours that Jesus cannot touch.

Luke's account runs slightly differently. After the final meal with his disciples, Jesus repairs to a familiar place, the Mount of Olives, where he was accustomed to go to pray. He goes there because he knows what is being asked of him: to take on the combined powers of sin and evil in a final and ultimate battle. He must prepare himself for this, and it will be a preparation for a struggle, a contest of strength. The strength called for, however, is not primarily physical, but inner, spiritual strength. And so he goes to the source of his strength, communion with God. It is a communion and a discipline with which he has been long familiar and to which he has become accustomed. But this contest will take extraordinary preparation. That God is with him to strengthen him is confirmed by the appearance of a divine emissary: an angel who, like an athletic trainer, guides him to the next level of preparation. At that point his communion with divine goodness and power is so intense that he is sweating like an athlete who is warming up to enter a contest at full strength. And he takes that sweating to its

ultimate point, where blood appears among the droplets of perspiration. Jesus is not exhausted; instead, he is now finally ready to
enter the ultimate combat.

The Matthean-Markan reading speaks to us of a spirituality in
which God understands our innermost struggles to discern and
obey, to do what we are called to do. The Lukan reading is a
spirituality of struggle—that is, a spirituality about the prayerful
discipline needed to enter into combat with evil and injustice in
situations of conflict. As many theologians and pastoral ministers
in Latin America have realized, the struggle against injustice requires more of them than strategies of liberation. It also takes a
spirituality of liberation, the cultivation of a relationship with God
that nourishes and directs the praxis of liberation.

What can the Lukan story tell us about spiritualities for conflict?
And more specifically, in what way is a spirituality of the blood of
Christ a spirituality for struggle? A number of things comes to
mind that might help us shape such a spirituality for today.

First of all, such a spirituality is not something that grows out of
occasional communion with God. In the training for athletic competition, one does not prepare for the contest by a single exercise
session. Endurance is built up only in gradual increments over a
long period of time. The mental concentration, and the coordination of mental concentration with physical exertion, take a considerable period of time. The athlete must train until the actions of
the contest become second nature, as it were, so that certain move-
ments come almost without thinking.

Jesus is pictured in the Gospel stories as one who not only is
active in his teaching and healing, but one who withdraws regularly for prayer. When faced with the supreme contest of his life,
Jesus withdraws once again for a final round of preparation. He
does not need the disciples for this; rather, he needs a familiar
space and routine wherein he can come into the closest possible
communion with his Father. The fact that he chooses as his place of
preparation a locale where he came often to pray helps reinforce
his preparation. It offers Jesus a sort of head start in the training
process.

In the struggles we face in our own lives, we often come into
conflictual situations—be they interpersonal or socio-political—in
which things happen quickly, even too quickly. There is no time to
think and reason carefully when we enter, say, the emergency room
of a hospital or find ourselves at a police line. What we must
depend upon at that point is our spiritual coordination, so to

speak. We must depend upon what we have already learned, now embedded deeply within our bodies and souls. When things happen quickly, reflexes count—reflexes that have been built up over a considerable period of time.

A spirituality for conflict is a kind of active waiting. It is a focusing of one's being in order to get beyond the diffuse character of ordinary, day-to-day living where many things distract us and lead us off in different directions. Active waiting helps redefine our perceptions. When one learns to concentrate, one discovers all sorts of things about the immediate environment not previously noticed. Active waiting redefines our geography, as it were. It makes us in the first instance more attentive to ourselves, helping us locate our centers of strength and our tattered edges of weakness. But active waiting also makes us more attuned to those whom we encounter. We experience less of our own "noise" created by inexact hearing and feeling, and we experience more the subtle manifestations of the other. It is a spirituality of watchfulness.

Jesus' comportment on the Mount of Olives showed him to be a master of such a spirituality. He moved through stages of preparation, first the more familiar and reflexive and then the less familiar and more difficult. As he entered the most difficult stages, he received special divine aid and encouragement. And finally he reached a new peak in the intensity of communion with God: Jesus prays to the point of blood. He has discovered the prayer that leads to blood.

This kind of prayer can be analyzed in two ways. It can be analyzed first of all in terms of intensity. Such prayer leads to the physical intensity of bloodshedding, a bursting of the bonds of the human body, a form of prayer unequalled in its centeredness. It strains the physical substratum of the subject to a point of inner explosion.

A second kind of analysis leads to recognition that such spiritual intensity is bound to attract and provoke the powers of sin and evil. Such powers have no choice but to engage Jesus; otherwise they will surely be overwhelmed. Those who follow in Jesus' way are bound to encounter the same opposition. The Letter to the Hebrews reflects this: "Remember how he [Jesus] endured the opposition of sinners; hence do not grow despondent or abandon the struggle. In your fight against sin you have not resisted to the point of shedding blood" (12:4).

A spirituality of struggle and conflict often counsels resistance rather than active combat, and resistance to evil often leads to certain consequences, as so many have learned in the world of today. The prayer of Jesus is prayer that leads to blood because it touches those deep and fundamental realities that shape human life and destiny, where the intensely spiritual touches the boundaries and limits of the physical. A spirituality of struggle and conflict is a spirituality of blood, for blood carries within it the intensities where life and death meet. When life and death encounter each other, there is bound to be struggle. Sometimes our posture in that struggle has to be one of resistance, perhaps the highest form of the active waiting discussed above. Sometimes it is marked by more active combat, at which point all the resources of the individual or the community must be so coordinated as to work as one being.

Luke's account reminds us that we cannot rush into the struggle like the hapless Peter, wielding a sword (22:50). We must prepare ourselves all along the way in prayer, the prayer that leads to blood. For without such preparation, the contests that confront us will find us quickly overwhelmed and lacking in endurance. The prayer that leads to blood reminds us of what ultimately may be demanded of us. It therefore also admonishes us about what we must do in looking toward that time: we must learn the subtle ways of resistance and be attuned to energies needed for struggle. We must learn active waiting, and develop the reflexes that sum up and focus our resources. Indeed, struggle can be carried out successfully only with a spirituality to support our efforts, and a spirituality of blood provides a prime way of preparing for such struggle.

The Cup of Suffering, the Cup of Blessing

Then, taking bread and giving thanks, he broke it and gave it to them, saying: "This is my body to be given for you. Do this as a remembrance of me." He did the same with the cup after eating, saying as he did so: "This is the new covenant in my blood, which will be shed for you." (Lk. 22:19–20)

This passage from the Gospel of Luke, with its parallels in the Gospels of Matthew and Mark, as well as in the First Letter to the Corinthians, is one very familiar to us: these words are repeated each time the eucharist is celebrated. In reflecting upon these words, the focus here will be upon Luke's version of them, but there will be references to parallel accounts as well.

Luke's Account: Setting and Specifics

The setting for these words is a meal Jesus has with his disciples. In the Gospel of Luke it is the eighth reference to Jesus' sharing a meal. A meal was an opportunity for Jesus to present the image of the banquet of heaven, the messianic banquet that will mark the presence of the reign of God. And the conversation during the meal also provided Jesus a forum for his teaching.

This meal, however, was to be a very special one. It was to be the celebration of Passover, commemorating God's deliverance of the Hebrews from the slavery of Egypt. At the time of Jesus, the Passover meal had also become a time of keen expectation of the coming of the Messiah who would free Israel from the yoke of foreign domination and restore its freedom.

Not only was it Passover, however. This meal was to be a final and farewell meal for Jesus, as he faced what he knew would be his arrest and condemnation. It would be his final testament to his disciples, a chance to sum up his teaching and to leave them his legacy. All four of the Gospels have the story of the Last Supper. The discourse in the Gospel of John is the longest (Jn. 13–17). All the Gospels have Jesus speaking as well as doing.

A word should be said also about the two cups of wine in Luke's version of the story. In the Passover celebration of Jesus' time, three cups of wine were shared around the table in the course of the meal. The first cup was offered at the very beginning of the meal, and was referred to as the *kiddush* cup. It was offered with a prayer, thanking God for the covenant with Israel. The second cup came after the *haggadah*, the telling of the Passover story. Then bread was blessed, broken, and shared around. At the end of the meal a final cup, the cup of blessing, was passed around after a prayer of thanksgiving. The two cups mentioned in verses 17 and 20 (Luke chap. 22) were probably the first and the third cups in this series.

What we have, then, is Jesus altering the traditional blessing of the bread and the third cup. The bread is no longer to be understood as merely bread shared, but as his body "given for you." The cup, blessing God and thanking God for the covenant, becomes a new covenant in the blood of Jesus, blood "which will be shed for you." This alteration of the ritual with the bread and the cup is always to be done thereafter as a way to remember Jesus. It is meant to sum up ritually and symbolically the message and mission of Jesus, a way of having Jesus present among his followers whenever they would gather to pray and to celebrate this memorial.

There are two distinctive elements in Luke's version. He is the only one to speak of the covenant in Jesus' blood as the *new* covenant. And Matthew and Mark say this blood is poured out for many, but Luke says that it is poured out for *you*.

With this as background, we are now in a position to examine a little more closely this story in order to see what resources it might provide for a spirituality of the blood of Christ. There are four elements here that deserve special attention in this regard:

1. the blood of the new covenant;
2. the blood poured out for you;
3. the cup of suffering;
4. the cup of blessing.

The Blood of the New Covenant

The Passover ritual, which pious Jews enacted each year, was not only a commemoration of the escape of the firstborn from the final plague in Egypt; it was also a celebration of God's covenant with the people in the Sinai wilderness (Ex. 24:3–8). So the commemoration had to do both with Israel's first experience with God as a saving God, and with the stirring event when Israel received the law and became God's special people. In the Passover meal, these events were celebrated by recounting the story in Exodus 12 and by the singing of the Hallel Psalms (Ps. 113–118).

Hence, the themes of rescue and covenant were closely intertwined. One could not comprehend the protection and rescue God had given the people in Egypt without understanding the commitment and promise that God gave in the Sinai covenant. And by the same token, the covenant was formed with a people not unknown to God—the people God had led out of Egypt.

It is within the commemoration of this complex of rescue and covenant that Jesus announces a new covenant. It is clearly meant to be in continuity with the Sinai covenant; its announcement is made within the very commemoration of that first covenant. Israel had experienced a succession of covenants and covenant renewals. But the one that Jesus now inaugurates can be compared only with that of Sinai. It is not a renewal, an extension, or a restoration of covenants once made; it is to be understood as foundational to the new age that was now upon Israel.

Jesus was announcing that the messianic age was coming upon Israel in his own person. The reign of God, which he had been preaching, was now to break upon them. It would be ushered in by a new covenant with God, and that was what Jesus was doing. The first covenant would not be commemorated again in the Passover ritual; instead, it would be celebrated in the messianic kingdom: "I have greatly desired to eat this Passover with you. I tell you I will not eat again until it is fulfilled in the kingdom of God" (Lk. 22:15–16).

A common motif running through the first and now this final covenant is their ritual sealing in blood. In the Sinai covenant the blood of young bulls was sprinkled upon the altar and the people. In this new and final covenant the blood of God's chosen emissary is drunk as the blessing cup, thanking God for this great gift of the covenant. The sharing of the cup bonds together those who partake of it in the new covenant of the messianic kingdom. It is a bold gesture, the offering of a cup of wine as blood. But it marks the depth of God's commitment in this new covenant. For the very life-force of God's chosen emissary now courses through the bodies of those who have accepted the invitation into the divine kingdom.

The stark character of Jesus' offer here—to come drink his blood—makes us realize that we are no longer talking about an ordinary people or an ordinary age. As was seen above in chapter 3, a basic law among the Jews was that drinking blood was forbidden, for blood was sacred to God. And to many non-Jews, the thought of drinking blood was simply repulsive. But what Jesus is saying is that the blood that belongs to God now belongs to the community of those who believe in Jesus and follow after him. The life-force of God is now with the disciples of Jesus in a special way.

For a spirituality of blood, Jesus' offer of his blood is an invitation to partake of the very life-force of God, to draw upon the deep wellsprings of divine life as sustenance for day-to-day existence. It is a proclamation of what resources of life we are able to bring to the continuing struggle between the forces of life and death in our world. And to partake of this blood is to be drawn into a community with the Lord, to be a member of God's people in a special way.

The Blood Poured Out for You

A striking feature of Luke's account is that Jesus says that this blood is poured out "for you" (or "for your sake"). The reference here is certainly to the sacrificial pouring out of blood for sealing a covenant. As we have seen, blood was a central symbol in Jewish ritual. It conveyed the sense of mediating between life and death, between the seen and the unseen world. Jesus' pronouncement here makes it clear that he is offering his own blood in place of the blood of a vicarious sacrificial animal.

But the context in which all of this takes place makes the offering of the cup something more than the sealing of a covenant, another communication of commitment and promise between God and the people. This all takes place as a final legacy of Jesus to his disciples before he undergoes his passion. The pall of imminent suffering hangs over the normally festive Passover celebration. By adding the words "for you" to his declaration, another dimension of meaning is added to the ritual. The sacrifice of which Jesus is a part is more than the sealing of a covenant; it also becomes a sin offering, expiating and forgiving the sins of his disciples.

From what we can reconstruct of the experience of the first disciples, it would appear that there was considerable evolution in their understanding of what the death of Jesus meant. Initially, it must have been a source of disappointment and even scandal for them. Jesus, who had preached as the final prophet of God, inaugurating God's reign and the restoration of Israel, had had his mission summarily and prematurely interrupted. He had been executed on charges either of sedition or of stirring up the people. Those who were associated with Jesus, therefore, ran the risk of being arrested and executed on the same charges. And the Gospel traditions all relate how the disciples abandoned Jesus during his suffering and fled. In the case of Peter, there was even an outright denial.

At that stage, at least, the disciples must have experienced Jesus' death as a profound disappointment. Perhaps, they thought, Jesus had even been wrong about speaking and acting on God's behalf, for the promised reign of God did not come upon them after his death. His death was a sign that God had abandoned him. This reaction to Jesus' death is reflected in the words of the disciples on the way to Emmaus: "We were hoping that he was the one who would set Israel free" (Lk. 24:21).

If the disciples did indeed think this way, such an attitude must not have lasted long. It seems likely that some, remembering Jesus' prophetic activities, came to understand his death not as a rejection by God, but the rejection and death that comes to all the prophets of God. There was a tradition to the effect that Israel rejected and murdered all its prophets (Lk. 6:23; 11:47–50), and Jesus would be seen as the latest in that line. Hence his death was not a rejection of his message, but a confirmation of it. Once again Israel had rejected the prophet of God. The rejection proved the veracity of Jesus' message.

But yet another understanding of Jesus' death came to prevail. In this view, perhaps under the influence of Jesus' own words at the Last Supper (if the words "for many" or "for you" do indeed go back to Jesus), the death of Jesus is to be interpreted in the light of the songs of the suffering servant to be found in Isaiah, especially in the fourth of those songs (Is. 52:13–53:12). In those songs, the servant of the Lord bears the infirmities and sins of the people, like the scapegoat on the Day of Atonement. The servant's life becomes a sin offering, and his death "shall take away the sins of many, and win pardon for their offenses" (Is. 53:12).

The "for many" in the Matthean and Markan formula, and the "for you" in Luke's version, evoked memories of the suffering servant for the early disciples of Jesus. Jesus' offering of his blood comes to have more than the usual communicative power of blood offered: it takes on pardoning and saving power as well. In other words, Jesus' death is no longer seen as an execution; instead, it is now seen as an act of sacrifice, whereby an alienated world is brought into communion with God.

It took a considerable leap to come to understand the death of Jesus as an act of sacrifice, an act that restored communication between God and the world. The sacrifice is at once the inauguration of a new covenant, and a sin offering and atonement. The blood bonds the world to God in a new covenant, and expiates and washes away the sin of the world.

This becomes a central way for the New Testament writers to understand the significance of Jesus' life and death. It has also served traditionally as the basis for a spirituality of the blood of Christ, especially in its expiatory and forgiving dimensions. It is possible that this notion of Jesus' death as sacrifice could go back to Jesus himself, in his words to his disciples at the Last Supper. Jesus, then, would have seen his own impending death as the apex of his prophetic activity rather than the ending of it. In this crowning achievement, Jesus himself became the sacrifice by which the reign of God would be brought about on earth.

The tradition that sees the eucharist as a sacrifice, strong especially in Catholic and Orthodox Christianity, has its foundation in this belief about Jesus' own self-understanding of what was to happen to him. Jesus' offering of his blood, and his injunction that his followers were ever to do the same, form the eucharistic dimension of a spirituality of the blood of Christ. Before this can be explored more fully, however, the symbolism of the cup needs to be examined.

The Cup of Suffering

In the Last Supper story, the fact that Jesus offers his own blood rather than the blood of a sacrificial animal is striking enough. But as we saw, he takes it a step further by inviting the disciples to partake directly of the blood from the cup he hands them. He brings together the symbolism of the cup with the symbolism of blood. To understand the full significance of Jesus' action here, the biblical meanings of the cup need our attention.

The cup has significance in both Testaments as a vessel for gathering and collecting. A cup of offering represented the drawing together of diverse elements, experiences, and emotions. The cup was also the vehicle by which those diverse elements, experiences, and emotions could be passed on to another. The Lukan passage reminds us of two aspects of the cup that Jesus offers: the cup of suffering and the cup of blessing.

The cup that Jesus offers—of his own blood "poured out for you"—is a cup that gathered together his destiny and especially his sufferings. This is reflected in a question he puts to the disciples at one point: "Can you drink of the cup I am to drink of?" (Mt. 20:22). In the episode in the garden immediately after the Last Supper, Jesus prays that the cup coming to him might pass away from him (Mt. 26:39; Lk. 22:42). The cup of suffering is also the cup filled with God's wrath (Rv. 14:10; 16:19). It is a cup of bitterness, and in accepting it from God, Jesus receives the destiny of his suffering and the accumulation of God's wrath that he must expiate.

The cup that Jesus offers his disciples at the Last Supper is a cup of suffering. To become a disciple of Jesus, to witness to the coming of God's reign, is to accept suffering, something the disciples were soon to find out. To have a share in that cup of suffering is to join in the struggle against Satan and the forces of evil and injustice that stalk society. It is a cup that should not be accepted lightly. Paul reminds the Corinthians that those who accept the cup unworthily are drinking it to their own condemnation (1 Co. 11:27).

The cup, the commemoration of the Lord's passion and death, has always been central to a spirituality of the blood of Christ. Reflection on the cup of suffering should remind us that, when we offer this cup in the eucharist, we are making some very strong commitments.

Those who preside at the eucharist and offer this cup, presenting it to the people during the eucharistic prayer and offering it to God in praise, must ask themselves: When we present this cup, can we stand worthily as individuals who can indeed sum up the sufferings of Christ's living body today—the church—and offer them to God? Are we in close enough solidarity with the suffering of the people to act as its representatives in this way?

And when eucharistic ministers and believers offer and receive the cup in communion, saying "the blood of Christ" and affirming it with "Amen," they must ask themselves: Are we ready to take on the sufferings of Christ's living body? Do we have the courage to offer that cup of suffering to one another, knowing that to follow Jesus will bring us into conflict and adversity? Holding up and receiving that cup is a commitment to sharing in deepest solidarity with the victims of this world—those who undergo pain, those who are oppressed, those who must await redemption. That cup is a reminder of the accumulated suffering that spans our lives and our societies, a cup that never seems to be emptied of its sorrows. What we do as Christians in the eucharist is one of the most moving aspects of the spirituality of the blood of Christ—the holding up of the cup of Christ's suffering, and sharing it among ourselves. It is an act that is not to be done casually, lest we drink it to our own condemnation.

The Cup of Blessing

The cup that Jesus offered his disciples at the Last Supper was a cup of suffering, but it was also a cup of blessing. When Jesus offered it to them, the Hallel Psalm would have still been ringing in their ears: "The cup of salvation I will take up, and I will call upon the name of the Lord" (Ps. 116:13). And for those committed to a spirituality of the blood of Christ, the words of Paul would come to mind immediately as well: "Is not the cup of blessing we bless a sharing in the blood of Christ?" (1 Co. 10:16).

The cup of blessing is a celebration and a thanksgiving for the covenant. That cup of blessing held up today in the eucharist is a celebration of the new covenant and the life it portends: a kingdom where justice shall prevail and every tear will be wiped away. It is a celebration of how much God's reign is already present among us. Just as the cup of suffering gathers together the suffering of the community, so the blessing cup brings together the deep joy and the happiness that come from being a disciple of the Lord. It is indeed a sharing and communion in the blood of Christ, a participation in the very life of God, now coursing through Christ's living body, the church.

Again, there are implications here for a spirituality of the blood of Christ. Just as we might question ourselves as to our worthiness and willingness to hold up the cup of suffering and to receive it and offer it to others, so too with the blessing cup. Do we live our own lives rooted in the joy of God, and are we in close enough solidarity with others to be part—really part—of their joys and thankfulness to God? Can we hold up that cup of blessing, receive it ourselves, and offer it to others, and be a blessing for them? Or are we outsiders, received among the poor and those who suffer more as visitors than as those who truly walk with them? For there are different qualities of participation in blessing. We can participate as guests, sharing in the graciousness of those who host us. Or we can participate more fully, by having walked with others through the events and experiences they now celebrate. The celebration of the blessing cup in this instance is a reaffirmation of the bonds that unite a community, a cup that holds within it both the pain and the pride of a people.

The eucharistic cup provides one of the most stringent tests of a spirituality of the blood of Christ. It tests our courage to confront and accept suffering, and it tests the quality of our participation in the fullness of life given to us in Christ. As Winfried Wermter has pointed out in his own reflections on the spirituality of blood, we are called upon to be "living chalices"—that is, the sufferings and joys of our world are poured into us, and our spiritual discipline must help us to grow into becoming both worthy and suitable receptacles for the events, experiences, and emotions of our world.

Conclusion

In the story of the Last Supper, a number of themes from the biblical tradition converge to forge a significant portion of a spirituality of blood. The covenant theme, with its overtones of creating new life and a new people, is conjoined to Jesus' heralding of the reign of God. In the coming of God's reign, a new covenant, a new relationship is upon us. But this event is more than a proclamation of covenant. It is also a sin offering, expiating the wrongdoings of the past and opening up new communion with God. The execution of Jesus is not to be seen as the tragic end of a misguided prophet, but as an act of sacrifice that inaugurates a new age. Jesus offers his disciples his body as nourishment and a cup that brings together within itself a complex history of suffering and hope. It is a cup that gathers together suffering and sin. But it is also offered in anticipation of the messianic banquet in heaven when all will be seated around God's table and there will be no more hunger. Jesus also enjoins his disciples to drink this blood, to participate directly in the life of God.

All these motifs converge in the Christian ritual of the eucharist. It is not surprising, then, that the eucharist has been such a source of comfort and strength to believers through the centuries. Its message is a bold one: an invitation to participate in the fullness of the life of Christ, but also a challenge to live in solidarity with those who suffer and to struggle for a better future with those who live in hope.

The full dimensions of a spirituality of the blood of Christ are not intelligible without understanding the eucharist. Along with covenant, it forms one of the central points in this spirituality. One must learn to accept the cup: a cup of suffering, a cup of blessing. In it are mingled the pain and the dreams of the world. From it comes strength for the struggle against pain and injustice, and from it comes the challenge to work in order to bring about God's reign. The cup of the blood of Jesus makes us participants both in the life of God and in the struggle against the suffering of the world.

Forgiveness through the Cross

It is precisely in this that God proves his love for us: that while we were still sinners, Christ died for us. (Rm. 5:8)

It is in the letters of Paul that the theological foundations for a spirituality of the blood of Christ are most clearly expressed. For it fell to Paul to plumb the meaning of Christ's death at a level without parallel elsewhere in the New Testament. What was one to make of the fact that Jesus' own ministry had been terminated abruptly and prematurely by his execution as a rabble-rouser? And why, given that fact, had the movement around him continued to grow rather than become dispersed, as had happened with other would-be prophets of the period? And if one looked at the meaning of all this as a committed member of the Jesus-movement and not simply as an interested observer, one would ask: Why was Jesus raised from the dead? What message lies in that unprecedented act of God for those who would follow Jesus?

In many ways, Paul occupied a unique position for grappling with these questions. For he had started as an interested—albeit hostile—observer of the movement around Jesus. Paul never knew Jesus of Nazareth; he was familiar only with the reactions of Jesus' disciples after Jesus' death. His own persecution of the Jesus-movement brought him into very close contact with it, a contact that would lead to his conversion.

Once he found himself a member of the community of Jesus and had experienced the call to go out and preach the good news about what God had done in Jesus, he had to ask those same questions about Jesus again, but this time from an insider's perspective. What was God trying to say by permitting Jesus' death on the cross and then by raising him up from the dead? Moreover, Paul found himself having to communicate his insights on this question to persons who, like himself, had had no opportunity for contact with the earthly Jesus of Nazareth. Paul became the apostle to those outside Judea and Galilee, to both Jews and gentiles. He had to try to make sense of God's activities for persons of his time and place. And he was the first to leave us a written record of his reflections in his letters.

It is perhaps for this reason that Paul's letters have always held such a special place for Christians. We too, like Paul, have not known Jesus of Nazareth in the flesh, but build our own faith on the testimony of those who have gone before us. We, too, must try to situate our experience of God's activity in our lives in relation to the message and ministry of Jesus, but at considerable remove from the time and place of Jesus. That Paul often opens up more suggestions than he is able to follow through; that he tries out images and analogies that take him a certain distance before—like all comparisons—they begin to limp; that he casts around for a wide variety of different ways of speaking of God's saving reality—all these efforts endear Paul to us, because they speak to our own quest for ways to give expression to what has moved us so deeply.

The reason why a spirituality of the blood of Christ is something that Christians would try to develop and live corresponds to Paul's own struggles to give voice to what was within him. The Western Middle Ages were to witness the development of a spirituality of the bloodsheddings of Christ that spanned the entire Passion story, but it is the shedding of the blood on the cross that gives the other bloodsheddings their legitimacy as a way of organizing our experiences of the meaning of Jesus Christ for us. And our first set of keys for unlocking that possibility is to be found in the Pauline letters.

The image of the blood of Christ is prominent in Paul's letters, although certainly not his prime or only image. His development of that image achieves several purposes. It takes an image already prominent in Jewish tradition and uses it to explain what God is now doing for that special, chosen people. It also plays out some of the larger, transcultural meanings of blood as a way of allowing both Jew and gentile to come to appreciate more fully what God has done in Jesus. And perhaps most radically, it helps connect that great scandal of Christian teaching—the scandal of the cross—to a larger tradition of religious experience.

This chapter and the following explore four ways in which Paul uses the imagery of the blood of Christ to explain God's saving activity. The two covered in this chapter stay close to the Jewish heritage that has been the basis for discussion here thus far. Paul makes important connections between the utterly secular, scandalous death of Jesus and a great sacral tradition, leading to the possibility of a new way of looking at that great heritage. In the next chapter, I study Paul as he pursues the image with vocabulary taken from his environment—words and meanings not necessarily dependent upon a background in the Jewish religious tradition. By so doing, Paul suggests how we can search our own environments for proper and compelling ways to speak of God's saving reality in our own time and place.

Both of these dimensions are important for a contemporary spirituality of the blood of Christ. For if this spirituality cannot relate to the great religious traditions from which it has sprung, then it has lost its memory and its roots. And if it cannot continue to find new forms in the manifold cultural settings of today's world church, it becomes a quaint and antiquarian bit of ecclesiastical lore that might prove charming, but certainly not compelling for the transformation of communities and cultures today.

In this chapter, then, there will be an exploration of Paul's speaking of salvation in Christ as expiation of sin and as justification. In the next chapter, I examine the experience of salvation as redemption and as reconciliation. By so doing, it is hoped that we will not only have a better appreciation of Paul's universe, but also discover the potential for expressing a contemporary spirituality of the blood of Christ grounded securely in the heart of Christian tradition.

Christ Our Expiation (Rm. 3:25)

"Through his blood," Paul tells us, "God made him [Jesus] the means of expiation for all who believe." In this terse sentence, Paul connects up the bloodshedding and death of Jesus on the cross with the sacred ritual of the Day of Atonement, when the high priest entered the Holy of Holies to seek forgiveness of sins for the people. In describing Jesus as "the means of expiation," Paul is equating Jesus' body with the propitiatory above the ark of the covenant in the sanctuary.

The propitiatory, as described in Exodus 25:17–22, was a plate of pure gold. It was mounted above the ark where the tablets of the law were kept. It was there, at the propitiatory, that the presence of God could be most keenly felt; and it was there that God would speak to the priest for the sake of the people. Thus, if there was any one place identifiable as the dwelling place of God on earth, it was the propitiatory.

For that reason, too, the propitiatory was sprinkled with sacrificial blood on the Day of Atonement. The blood was the vehicle of communication between the people and God, conveying with it the remorse of the people for sin and, as a sign of the life-force that belonged to God, the purifying forgiveness of God extended to a sinful people.

Paul makes a daring equation when he identifies Christ's crucified body with the propitiatory, and the blood of Christ with the sacrificial blood that brings about the forgiveness of sin. As we have seen, Jesus' death by crucifixion could only have been a source of scandal and shame to his followers. Crucifixion as a form of execution was reserved to convicted criminals who threatened harm to the state. Being stripped and hanged on the cross robbed the criminal of the last vestiges of human dignity. Had Jesus been stoned to death on charges of heresy or blasphemy, at least then the meaning of his message and ministry would have been acknowledged: his claims to speak on behalf of God and to herald the restoration of Israel in the coming reign of God would have at least been recognized, even if repudiated. But instead, Jesus had been handed over to the civil authorities and ordered to be put to death for causing a public disturbance. His prophetic claims were swept aside as irrelevant to the matter at hand, apart from the mocking inscription proclaiming him king of the Jews.

As was noted in chapter 6, early Christians struggled to comprehend the meaning of Jesus' death, if indeed it could be given any meaning at all. Was Jesus' life simply terminated abruptly, or was there a reason for his ignominious death? Did he die because Israel murdered all its prophets (as an oral tradition of the time had it)? Or was Jesus' death somehow part of his message rather than simply the end of it?

In this passage in the Letter to the Romans, Paul asserts boldly that the death of Jesus was part of the message he came to proclaim. Jesus was to be identified with the suffering servant of the Book of Isaiah, the servant who took upon himself the sins of the people as did the scapegoat on the Day of Atonement. As we saw in looking at the Last Supper texts, this interpretation of the death of Jesus may indeed go back to Jesus himself. At any rate, Paul extends the meaning of this association of Jesus and the suffering servant even further by identifying Jesus with the propitiatory and identifying the cross with the Holy of Holies in the temple. In making this bold association, Paul creates a new vision of the death of Jesus, and the meaning of Jesus' ministry. There are a number of points here that deserve our close attention.

First of all, in associating the body of Jesus with the propitiatory, Paul is asserting how intimately God dwells in Jesus. Christians were, of course, to develop this assertion more fully in their affirmation of the very divinity of Jesus. But in this assertion here Paul is saying that God dwells most intimately in a stripped, beaten, broken, and misunderstood man, condemned as a criminal and public nuisance. In other words, God is most completely revealed to us where we would least expect it. Rather than affirming values held as essential by society or revealing the divine presence at the center of public interest, God appears out on the fringes, in situations and actions beyond the pale of established values and ideals. God appears among the detritus of society, that which has been rejected and cast off. What this means is that God can best be comprehended among the broken and rejected rather than among the powerful and respected. God's dwelling place is not in some sanctuary cut off from the realities of a conflictive world; God dwells in the midst of the strident cries of those who are broken and call out for justice and mercy.

Secondly, by identifying Jesus with the propitiatory, the cross becomes by implication the Holy of Holies rather than an instrument of shame and public execution. Throughout his writings Paul speaks eloquently about the cross and the crucified Christ as "a stumbling block to Jews, and an absurdity to Gentiles; but to those who are called, Jews and Greeks alike, Christ the power of God and the wisdom of God" (1 Co. 1:23–24). Paul boasts of nothing but the cross of Christ (Ga. 6:14). By claiming the cross as the privileged place of God's dwelling on earth, Paul opens up a grand paradox at the very heart of our perception of the world and of reality. Where we would think that goodness and completeness dwell—above or beyond the fray of daily existence—is not the place to look for them at all. Goodness and completeness dwell beyond the reach of power, beyond reliance on one's own strength, beyond access to abundant resources. Goodness and completeness dwell in that broken and shamed figure hanging on an instrument of execution. Somewhere in the midst of that violent ending of life lies the hope for new life. Somewhere in the gesture of powerlessness of one stretched out on the cross lies genuine power. Somewhere in the shame of a body stripped and exposed to public ridicule lies the beginnings of true human dignity.

All the values thought to hold a society together are turned on their head. The cross becomes the sign of this dramatic reversal of values and ideals. To embrace suffering, rather than avoid it, becomes the way to wholeness. Losing control, rather than struggling to maintain control at every turn, becomes the means to true power. Facing conflict rather than avoiding it becomes the way to redemption. And what seemed to be the tragic dashing of dreams is the dawn of the reign of God.

Unfortunately, Christians have spent as much time trying to avoid the cross as they have preaching and embracing it. The message of the cross on where to find God is hard to accept. It was a scandal to Jews and an absurdity to Greeks, Paul reminds us. And what is it to Christians of today?

Thirdly, Paul identifies the shedding of Jesus' blood with the expiatory blood of the Day of Atonement. The violence inherent in Jesus' shedding of blood in his execution is compared here with the blood sprinkled on the propitiatory. What Paul is saying is that the execution of Jesus is not the termination and rejection that it might appear to be. It is instead a saving action, a forgiveness of human sin marking the new age of the reign of God. Jesus' blood, shed in violence, creates a new life out of the ruins of a human life. It is not blood hapazardly shed; it is an act of death that brings about life. Paul says that one can come to understand the true meaning of the blood of Jesus only by comparing it to the most sacred ritual action of his heritage, the Day of Atonement. A new sacrality is established here, redefining what is to be considered holy and what is to be considered ordinary.

Thus, within the narrow confines of this sentence in Romans 3:25, Paul redefines the way we are to seek God and approach our world. The blood shed by Christ on the cross creates a new center of the sacred in our world; it reorients us as to where we might find God and the fullness and completeness we seek. The blood shed in the execution of Jesus becomes the vehicle for conveying to us a new existence, a new age. It becomes a saving blood, overcoming the violence and death-dealing powers of the world to herald the reign of God among us. It becomes a rescuing blood, unloading from our backs the consequences of our own sin and the sins of others heaped upon us.

What does all this mean for a spirituality of the blood of Christ? By relocating the dwelling place of God in the world, and by redefining the violent death of Jesus as the means whereby God opens up a new age by the forgiveness of sins, a new orientation is given to those who would follow Jesus. If the blood of the covenant and the blood of the cup were two of the supporting points of a spirituality of the blood of Christ, the third is the blood of the cross. Those who would follow Christ in a spirituality of blood always have before them the cross: the cross both as the new sanctuary of God and as a symbol of the violence and suffering that stalk our world. The blood of the cross reminds us where God is to be found most clearly: among the rejected, the powerless, the despised, the imprisoned. And it reminds us, too, that there is a way out of the suffering and the violence that scar individual human lives and entire societies. The blood of the cross promises ultimate release from a world filled with injustice and suffering. And it promises strength to those who now shed their own blood, who learn how to share in Christ's sufferings by being formed into the pattern of his death (Ph. 3:10). The sufferings we undergo need no longer point us only to the void of oblivion and death. Through the blood of the cross, our sufferings can be drawn into that sacred circle where the cross of Christ stands, where the holiness of God truly dwells.

The expiating blood of the cross releases us from sin—the sins that have skewed our individual histories and the sins that have twisted our societies. That expiating blood, like the blood of the Day of Atonement, allows us to begin with refreshed histories, allows us to enter a new age as new persons.

Paul's vision of the expiating blood of Chirst offers an important resource to a spirituality for conflictual situations. By its redefining the dwelling place of God in the world, it helps avoid mistaking human power and oppressive force for the power of God. Those who find themselves championing the oppressed in conflict do not draw their energy and strength from the same source as do oppressors. Paul's vision enables the oppressed to define their world differently, and bring redemptive grace into the heart of conflict. To meet oppressors on their own terms means that the oppressed could well become the next generation of oppressors, continuing the rotation of the wheel of injustice. But if the true dwelling place of God is recognized, sin can be expiated. The blood of the cross becomes the sign and reminder of where the power and grace of God are to be sought.

Christ Our Justification (Rm. 5:9)

In Romans 5:9 Paul says: "now that we have been justified by his blood, it is all the more certain that we shall be saved by him from

God's wrath." If the passage just discussed saw the death of Jesus in association with the most solemn of religious rituals, in this passage Paul tries to grasp what God has done in Jesus in terms of a court of law. To be justified here means to be cleared of any wrongdoing, to be found righteous. The image Paul presents us, then, is one of coming before God as before a judge in a court of law. Inasmuch as no human is blameless before God, for we have all sinned (Rm. 5:12), we stand convicted by our own deeds. We are bound to feel upon our necks the scorching heat of God's wrath.

But Christ makes us righteous through the shedding of his blood. What does this mean? It has to be understood, first of all, in connection with the passage on expiation in Romans 3:25. Christ's shedding of blood on the cross has expiatory power for our offenses. As a result, we can now stand before the tribunal of God's judgment as righteous, and escape the punishment that might have been ours.

This image of our being justified through the blood of Christ just as an accused person might be declared innocent before the law seems a somewhat legalistic way of considering our relationship to God. For many, in meditating on this passage, this talk of justification before God's wrath gets mixed up with Christian antipathy toward the Mosaic law, a law from which the gospel liberates. But as the reflections in chapter 2 tried to emphasize, to dismiss the use of legal language from the discussion of salvation may be a narrow-minded strategy. Not to want to use legal imagery is a most natural reaction for persons who live in societies where the rule of law is respected. To speak in legal language, then, seems somewhat superfluous or even superficial. Of course—someone might say in such a situation—we live *with* law, but it is not the language with which to express the higher aspects of who we are. Law is something to be taken for granted.

But for those who do not live in societies where the rule of law is respected, the perspective can be quite different. When human lives and destinies are decided arbitrarily by dictators, or when military juntas replace the courts of law in arbitrating the present and future, then law emerges in its fullness as the basic ordering that makes us human. The Hebrew celebration of the law in the Book of Exodus is an example. As slaves, they had no rights and no recourse to the law for protection from those more powerful than themselves. But in the law given them by God, they took on a new dignity. Their rights were affirmed and respected.

Thus to speak of our relationships with God in terms of law is to say that God takes us and our actions seriously. It is to say that God does not treat us arbitrarily, nor does God allow things to happen through sheer caprice. It means that there is order and meaning to things and events.

Seen in this way, God takes our sinfulness seriously, and also takes our justification seriously. Through the expiating blood of Christ, we can come to stand before God and partake in the fullness of relationship to God. Our past is forgiven and forgotten; we can begin anew.

A second aspect of Romans 5:9 that some find alienating is the reference to the appeasement or escaping of God's wrath. When we realize that this has been achieved through the shedding of Christ's blood, it can make God seem like some sadistic, bloodthirsty deity who has to be appeased by human sacrifice. That might have been a defensible reading of this passage had verse 8 not preceded it. There Paul says: "It is precisely in this that God proves his love for us: that while we were still sinners, Christ died for us."

Paul frames the discussion of justification in a discussion of God's great love for us. Christ's death, then, cannot be understood as a violent act demanded by a vengeful God. It is rather the free and loving response of Jesus to bring human beings into a justified communication with a God who loves them deeply, but is alienated from them out of respect for their own autonomy under the law. In this way of thinking, the expiatory death of Jesus is not something laid upon Jesus as it might have been laid upon an unwilling scapegoat. It is an expiatory death freely undertaken, as a death for the sake of one's friends (Jn. 15:13; Rm. 5:7). Love, then, is the motivating force, not vengeance.

What does this reflection on the justifying blood of Christ mean for a spirituality of blood? It means that the blood of Christ is a sign of the great dignity God accords human life and the great seriousness with which God takes human actions. The blood of Christ proclaims human dignity even when it is denied in an inhuman society. Because God has cared to see us justified, those who do not respect that basic dignity will come to feel the wrath of God. The blood of Christ is the sign of God's respect for human dignity, especially in those situations where that dignity is not accorded the respect that is its due.

The blood of Christ is also a reminder to the righteous that we have all been sinners, and it is only through the gracious love of God that the righteous have attained justification. Hence, those who would live by a spirituality of blood cannot content themselves with focusing on rescuing the oppressed; their purview must include the redemption—not the vanquishing—of oppressors as well. The blood of Christ is a reminder of the dignity that God accords even to sinners and those not considered righteous. As Paul reminds us, Christ did not die for us when we were justified, but when we were still sinners.

Conclusion

In these two passages from Romans, Paul draws lines from two of the most fundamental aspects of his religious experience—the Day of Atonement and the giving of the law—to the event of Jesus' execution on the cross. In doing this, the bloodshedding of Jesus takes on new and powerful meaning. It does not remain the violent and seemingly senseless termination of an individual's life; it assumes a cosmic significance, becoming an event with meaning for the whole of history. The cross relocates the center of the sacred in the world, and Jesus' body becomes the dwelling place of divinity. The blood of Christ becomes the vehicle of ritual communication that expiates wrongdoing and reaffirms human dignity. That lonely hill outside Jerusalem becomes the gateway to a new age, to a new existence where restored and intimate communication with God makes of erstwhile sinners and the lowly of this earth new women and men, living under the reign of a gracious and loving God.

In this perspective, the angle from which the struggle for justice is viewed and by which conflictual situations are entered is changed. From the perspective of the cross, one no longer concentrates only on survival and victory of the oppressed; expiation of the sinful roots of an oppressive situation and forgiveness of oppressors are included.

For those who experience suffering and injustice in the world in which they now live, this is a message of great power and comfort. It promises that sufferings now endured are not necessarily to be the totality of their existence; rather, they can become a pathway out of injustice and pain into a new reality. For in conforming our own pain to the pattern of Christ's death, we will come to share in the power of his resurrection (Ph. 3:10).

The blood of Christ stands as the sign that this promise can be fulfilled in us. It is the blood of the suffering Christ that will make of our sufferings something more than the disintegration of our bodies and the crumbling of our spirits. It is the blood of Christ that affirms our dignity before God even when the society in which we live denies us that dignity. The cross stands as the paradox of God's revelation about where divine presence is to be found and to whom divine grace has been imparted. And it is in the blood shed on that cross that we are made whole.

Our Redemption and Reconciliation

The last chapter examined some of the salvation vocabulary that Paul brought out of his own religious background, and then applied to what had happened to Jesus. This chapter continues that investigation of Paul, but moves to words taken from the secular context in which Paul lived.

Paul did not restrict himself to traditional religious language when speaking of the meaning of the death of Jesus. What God had done in Jesus was unprecedented. It exceeded the capacity of any of the familiar ways of talking about God's saving activity to express adequately the significance of this event. Yet Paul, as any other individual living in a concrete time and place, had to use language familiar to those in his environment if he wanted to be understood. And so he cast around for a variety of ways to give expression to this great event, looking also to the ordinary, day-to-day expressions of Mediterranean culture.

This suggests that we need to be attentive not only to the salvation language handed down to us as part of Christian faith, but also to how salvation is talked about in the world around us. One of the great failures of Christians is that they restrict themselves too closely to their traditional religious language. What often results from this is that God's saving activity seems distant and abstract to others, and therefore of little consequence. But if we examine Jewish and Christian traditions closely, it soon becomes apparent that many of the terms used for salvation began referred originally to concrete realities. It is only the distance of time and place that make them seem abstract to us today. Thus for the Hebrews, salvation meant escaping slavery in Egypt. It also meant long life, descendants, good health, and happiness. All these can be understood very concretely.

Today, concrete talk about salvation is most evident in places like Latin America, where salvation has to involve liberation from poverty and from oppressive political and economic structures. Many have been quick to point out that religious salvation cannot be equated with such earthly realities. This is true, but what kind of salvation would it be if it does not transform an oppressed day-to-day existence?

A spirituality of the blood of Christ requires an especially keen awareness of where salvation is needed, where there is a cry for liberation in our world today. It is not a matter of going around with a religious answer in the hopes that someone will ask the right question. It grows out of the symbol of blood itself. The symbol is not just about life, it is also about the death that roams the world. The blood of Christ is about salvation, about redeeming the suffering of the world. Hence the human quest for salvation is something that cannot be ignored in this spirituality.

This chapter examines two ways of talking about salvation that Paul borrowed from his environment. This is done not only to understand the biblical heritage more fully; it is also done as a guide for the contemporary quest to understand how God's saving activity touches our lives. The two terms that will be examined here are redemption and reconciliation.

Redeemed in Christ (Ep. 1:7–8)

The word "redemption" as a way of talking about salvation comes principally out of a secular background, although for Jews it had some religious overtones as well. The Greek word Paul used was *apolytrosis*, which means to release from bondage by ransom. The root of the word is *lytron*, which means ransom. The term was used in Mediterranean society to describe the freeing of slaves by buying their freedom. For Jews, the word evoked memories of their ancestors' being freed from slavery in Egypt.

It could be argued that another adequate translation of the Greek term would be "liberation," a translation that would favor the aspect of freeing the one held captive (the word *lytron* comes from the verb *luein*, which means to bind).

The word "redemption" has a Latin origin, and means literally "to buy back," thus capturing the ransom aspect of the Greek term.

Redemption has been something of a favored term for talking about salvation in Catholic theology, probably because of the influence of St. Anselm. Yet it is not all that common in the New

Testament. It does not appear in Luke, John, the pastoral Epistles, or Revelation. And it appears in Matthew and Mark only twice. It is Paul who uses this term most frequently.

And for Paul it had a particular power. In the communities around the eastern Mediterranean where he preached, a good number of the Christians he would have encountered would have been either slaves or freed slaves. The Book of Philemon is evidence of this. Thus to compare what God had done in Jesus to the experience (or for those still slaves, the hope) of freedom from the bondage of slavery would have been understood immediately.

There are a number of passages that associate this use of the language of redemption with the blood of Christ. In Ephesians 1:7–8 Paul describes the death of Jesus as a redemptive event: "It is in Christ and through his blood that we have been redeemed and our sins forgiven, so immeasurably generous is God's favor to us." In following out the analogy between Jesus' death and the ransoming of slaves, the blood of Christ becomes the ransom-price. The First Letter of Peter describes it even more graphically:

> Realize that you were delivered from the futile way of life your fathers handed on to you, not by any diminishable sum of silver or gold, but by Christ's blood beyond all price: the blood of a spotless, unblemished lamb, chosen before the world's foundation and revealed for your sake in these last days. (1:18–20)

There is a move here away from talking about the blood of Christ as sacrificial blood (although the text in 1 Peter tries to keep the connection) to blood as a ransom-price.

In the course of Christian history, Paul's analogy of the death of Christ with the manumission of slaves has been stretched further than Paul probably intended. There have been extensive discussions about who was paid the ransom. Was it the devil, who was holding sinners bondage? Or was it God? The orthodox position has been, of course, that God could not be beholden to the devil in any way, and that therefore the ransom had to be paid to God. When Anselm began to work out a theory of redemption in the eleventh century, he picked up especially on the Pauline language, but cast it in a legal context rather than one of slavery. His work has influenced the way Western Christianity has spoken of salvation down to the present day.

But it seems important not to press the analogy too far. To my mind, Paul was trying to make two points by introducing the language of redemption as a way of talking about the death of Jesus. First of all, those who experienced conversion to Christ Jesus had an experience of being released from their former state of existence. When that former state of existence was viewed from the perspective of life in Christ, it looked like a state of bondage, and could best be compared with the experience of slavery. Inasmuch as there were freed slaves in the community, that image was vivid and could be readily understood.

Secondly, if Christians had been redeemed from the bondage of sin, they no longer belonged to that world. They had been re-deemed to God—they now belonged to God rather than to the world of sin. So the language of ransom made them ask the question: To whom have we been ransomed? To whom do we now belong?

The ransoming was achieved through the blood of Christ. As such, it could evoke memories of sacrifice for Jewish members in Paul's audience. But it also could be understood as ransom in the sense of mediation or go-between. In other words, Jesus interposed himself between God and sin, between the powers of life and the powers of death. Blood, which mediates between life and death, is the prime symbol of what Jesus has done in pouring out his life for the sake of others. He pledged his own blood so that the blood of others need not be shed.

When ransoming is approached in this manner, Jesus' act of mediation in our behalf shows forth God's great love. Ephesians 1:8 certainly captures this in its linking redemption through Christ's blood with God's immeasurable generosity. That God would want so much to rescue us from the powers of sin and death in order to make of us a special people belonging to the world of life and to God bespeaks a deep and enduring love. The experience of being ransomed from the bondage of sin and of being gathered into God's embrace could be compared only to the exhilaration of achieving freedom.

When viewed from this perspective, it becomes clearer why redemption has been one of the prime ways of talking about salva-tion. It combines the experience of rescue and release from bond-age and the theme of God's great love. And humanity, in all its finitude, will continue to experience situations that cry out for rescue and release.

What does the language of redemption mean for us today? As was noted above, the Western Church has inherited a concept of redemption to explain what God has done in Jesus. That concept has been mediated to us principally through the work of Anselm, who described redemption in terms of a legal exchange, combining, as it were, the biblical notions of redemption and justification. But the most exciting contemporary development in our use of the language of redemption has come out of Latin America with its development of the concept of liberation. In the works of liberation theologians who use this word theologically, it appears that liberation is an adequate translation for *apolytrosis*. When used theologically, liberation is defined by the concrete circumstances and the effects of sin from which peoples need to be rescued. And liberation necessarily refers to the whole person and the whole community, and generally cannot be classified tidily into categories such as political or religious liberation. At the same time, of course, a careless equation of any kind of liberation with liberation from sin should be avoided. But more importantly, to realize the social consequences of sin and to realize the need to be rescued from those consequences is something that cannot be set aside as purely political or economic and therefore irrelevant to a Christian notion of salvation. Hence we can look to situations of poverty and conflict in our world as a privileged place for coming to understand what the biblical concept of redemption means for us today.

A clearer understanding of Paul's concept of redemption helps also in understanding phrases such as "redemptive suffering." With Paul's thought as background, redemptive suffering would mean suffering that is not destructive of the human person and community. It is suffering placed within the context of Christ's suffering (Ph. 3:10), and so is either directed to a purification of those suffering or is considered an opportunity for growth in wisdom or compassion. Redemptive suffering, then, is suffering that has been transformed, a suffering that becomes a vehicle for the elevation of the human spirit. What is important here is the redirection of suffering away from its natural tendency to destroy or dehumanize toward the goal of transformation to a fuller humanity.

What does Paul's understanding of redemption have to say to a spirituality of the blood of Christ? To speak of Christ's redeeming blood has been one of the principal ways of talking about salvation. There is a long tradition of speaking of the blood of Christ as the price of our redemption. What is of interest to us here are additional possibilities. Given what has been said here about the biblical meaning of redemption, a spirituality of this redeeming blood would be a spirituality willing to mediate the boundary between life and death. It would be a spirituality of the go-between, finding a way to translate the death-dealing events of a society into a resource for life. Such a spirituality of mediation helps define, too, the position of those who enter conflict for the sake of justice— seeking the redemption of an entire situation.

A spirituality of the redeeming blood of Christ would be a spirituality witnessing to God's great love for humankind by the pouring out of our own life for the sake of overcoming sin and suffering in our world (Rm. 5:8). It would be a spirituality that would proclaim redemption and work for its coming about: not redemption as some abstract and distant concept, but redemption here and now from the bondage of sin and the consequences of sin.

Brought Near through the Blood of Christ (Ep. 2:13–14)

Another image Paul used in speaking of the meaning of the death of Christ was that of reconciliation. Reconciliation was not a term used for salvation in the Hebrew scriptures. The term is a purely secular one. In its root, the Greek word means "to make peace after war." In Paul's time, it had become a technical word to describe the resolving of differences between husband and wife, a meaning still used in divorce courts today. It has overtones of bringing together what had been divided or separated, and the peace that ensues once that bringing together has taken place. In other words, the use of the word "reconciliation" in Paul's time was not much different from the use of the term today. The reconciliation needed after the damage of war or after the emotional trauma of the separation of spouses is a reality familiar to us.

There are two Pauline texts that relate reconciliation to the blood of Christ in a special way. One is Colossians 1:19–20: "It pleased God to make absolute fullness reside in him and, by means of him, to reconcile everything in his person, both on earth and in the heavens, making peace through the blood of his cross." The other is Ephesians 2:13–14: "But now in Christ Jesus you who once were far off have been brought near through the blood of Christ. It is he who is our peace, and who made the two of us one by breaking down the barrier of hostility that kept us apart."

In the text from Colossians Jesus becomes a point of cosmic reconciliation: all that has been divided and separated, in any time and in any place, is brought back together again. For in Jesus dwells absolute fullness—that is, the plenitude of divine life. And it is the blood of the cross that has achieved this, uniting human life with the divine life.

This is a grand vision, imaging the dissolution of every kind of alienation in the universe and the reunion of humanity with God. It has long been one of the favored images of salvation in the Eastern churches. The blood of Christ, the life-force of one filled with the divine life, becomes the principle whereby this great reconciliation is achieved. We have already seen Paul's understanding of the cross as the new dwelling place for God, the new Holy of Holies. The blood shed in that holiest of places becomes the means for overcoming death, infusing the world with divine life. And the result is peace—the peace experienced when war ceases, and when human lives and communities are no longer torn apart.

But to understand this cosmic reconciliation, Colossians reminds us that it must be kept in close contact with the expiating and expunging blood of the cross. The reconciliation spoken of here is not achieved by ignoring or sidestepping the sources of alienation; rather, they must be acknowledged and redeemed. Memories of violence cannot be repressed; they must be lifted up and healed. The cross keeps the reality of alienation and injustice before us. And to achieve genuine reconciliation, to break free of the webs and networks of oppression, the healing will need to be cosmic in nature—that is, "on the earth and in the heavens."

In a spirituality of the blood of Christ, this vision of ultimate reconciliation can serve as a source of strength for those who struggle to achieve reconciliation in a strife-torn world. Our attempts at overcoming what keeps us apart are often not very successful. When one thinks of the grinding poverty that most human beings experience as their daily lot, or the prospects of overcoming the acts of terror to which individuals have turned out of desperation, or the escalating spiral of acquisition of nuclear weaponry, the achieving of reconciliation seems a hopeless task. Reconciliation means the peace that comes after warfare, but we often find ourselves unable even to bring about an end to outright conflict.

Although we may believe that the fullness of divine life dwelling in Jesus has been given in the shedding of his blood, the realization of that fullness can seem very far away. The cosmic vision of the hymn in Colossians 1 can keep us from sinking away into despair by reminding us that the great reconciling work has already begun in Jesus. It reminds us, too, that the means whereby that reconciliation will be achieved is the cross. In other words, reconciliation cannot be achieved without considerable pain and a death to some of the things we deem important or hold dear. The blood of Christ is our share in the divine life that can sustain us in the long journey ahead of us.

In the passage from Ephesians, the image of bringing together in reconciliation is set out even more graphically. The division to be overcome here is that between gentile and Jew. The barrier of hostility referred to in the text was a three-meter-high barricade separating the inner and outer courts of the temple. Gentiles were not allowed beyond that barrier under pain of death. Ephesians presents the bringing together of gentile and Jew through the reconciling blood of Christ. The gentile had been held at a distance and now was not only allowed to draw near, but is actually brought closer. Again, as in the cosmic vision in Colossians, it is the blood of Christ, vehicle of the divine life-force, that effects this reconciliation.

This passage from Ephesians has come to be understood as reaching beyond the first-century reconciliation of gentile and Jew. It has become a paradigm of the reconciliation of humanity and God. Understood here is that the greater part of the reconciliation has to take place on the side of humanity. For humanity had lost its ability to feel the great love of God, and it took the activity of Jesus to bring about an awareness of this great love and of the reconciliation needed.

What does this passage offer us by way of a spirituality of the blood of Christ? If the passage from Colossians gives us a cosmic vision of ultimate reconciliation and the strength to endure the struggle until that reconciliation arrives, the text from Ephesians makes us focus on the concrete tasks of reconciliation before us. In the Ephesians text, the task is reconciliation of gentile and Jew. In our own situations, the reconciliation will take on other forms. The reconciliation of warring elements within Chile envisioned by the bishops of that country is one example. The reconciliation of peoples in countries like Guatemala or Peru in the wake of marauding death squads is another. And the reconciliation needed within families is something that has touched Christian communities everywhere. Reconciliation is difficult work, but our confidence in the blood of Christ inspires us to continue to struggle in the difficult and seemingly impossible situations that often face us.

Conclusion

In this chapter we have explored two dimensions of Paul's understanding of salvation and of the blood of Christ. The two concepts of redemption and reconciliation were drawn from secular society to help explain what God had done for the world in the death of Jesus on the cross. As was noted at the beginning of this discussion, such reaching out for concepts in the environment around us is something encouraged by what Paul has done. To some extent, the development of the concept of liberation in recent years is an example of this. The concern for economic justice and freedom from nuclear tyranny voiced by the U.S. Catholic bishops provide other examples. In any event, we need to be attuned in a special way to the possibilities offered us.

For a spirituality of the blood of Christ, redemption and reconciliation are very useful concepts for plumbing more deeply the symbolism of blood. Redemption helps us see how the saving power of his blood can transform what seems to be an utterly destructive situation of suffering or oppression into something that can elevate the human spirit rather than drag it down. Reconciliation looks to a cessation of the hostility and conflict that keep individuals and communities apart. It is a vision of the life-force in Christ's blood finally triumphing over the forces of death. Such a realization may seem far away, but Christians believe that the process has already begun in the reconciling death of Christ, and that the peace his cross will bring is even now beginning to come upon us.

9

Filling Up the Sufferings of Christ

Even now I find my joy in the suffering I endure for you. In my own flesh I fill up what is lacking in the sufferings of Christ for the sake of his body, the Church. (Col. 1:24)

A ny spirituality that hopes to provide an adequate framework for the exercise of Christian discipleship has to come to terms with the place and meaning of suffering in human life. For many persons in the world today, suffering is not an occasional incursion into their lives; it is an overwhelming feature of their day-to-day existence. For those who wake up each morning knowing they will face racial hostility as soon as they close their front door behind them; for those in whom the gnawing ache of hunger is never stilled; for those who live in unending fear under oppressive political regimes—suffering is a central part of their very lives.

Others, too, are subjected to long periods of suffering in their lives: those who have lost a loved one and are now alone; those who must bear the burden of chronic and painful illness; those who live under abiding and debilitating stress or depression. All of these have etched upon them the open wound of suffering.

And for still others, suffering comes suddenly and tears the fabric of their routines asunder. Sudden illness or accident, the pain of betrayal or abandonment, the dislocation of radically changed circumstances—these, too, bring with them a feeling of being wrenched out of normal existence.

Suffering winds its way through all our lives, and worms its way through the most careful of defenses. Cultures of abundance, such as those of Europe and North America, devote a great deal of their resources to keep suffering at arm's length. But despite advanced medical technology, refined psychotherapeutic techniques, and carefully constructed environments, suffering still finds its way into life: certain diseases still admit of no cure, the desperate still seek respite in suicide, and adolescents continue to flee from the most privileged of homes.

An adequate Christian spirituality must offer some resources for coping with suffering. It must provide more than a way to deny or elude the pain that comes upon us.

The theme of suffering is certainly a central one in a spirituality of the blood of Christ. As has been emphasized over and over again throughout this book, the symbol of blood gains its power from the fact that it represents within itself the forces of both life and of death. It is a celebration of the vigor of life and attendant blessings—love, community, justice, and hope; and it also acknowledges the dark side of existence—suffering, violence, and death.

A spirituality of the blood of Christ brings forward the mystery of suffering and death in the symbol of the cross, standing as a sign of the contradictions that mark our existence—contradictions about what constitute power and weakness, success and failure. The cross serves as a constant reminder of the failure of human goodness; but it also stands as the special place where God has chosen to dwell among the inhabitants of the earth. A sign of violence and disintegration of human life, it is also the pledge of a redemption from sin and suffering.

As was noted earlier, the cross stands with the covenant and the cup as the prime symbols by which the meaning of the blood of Christ is conveyed to us. Together they represent the fullness to which a spirituality of the blood of Christ calls those who believe. If separated or pursued in isolation from one another, things get out of balance. To speak of life and love in the symbol of the covenant without remembering the cross is to speak superficially or even naively about what human life is really all about. For the fruits of suffering borne in patience bring wisdom to human existence. But by the same token, living in suffering without the bonding of love and human community is destructive of human beings; it is life without hope, making a dehumanizing dead end of our days.

In searching the scriptures for a better understanding of this interplay between happiness and suffering, there is a passage in the Letter to the Colossians, 1:24, that is puzzling, at least when first encountered. Paul writes; "In my own flesh I fill up what is lacking in the sufferings of Christ."

What does Paul mean here by filling up what is lacking in the sufferings of Christ? Is he trying to say that the saving activity of Christ in his suffering and death was somehow incomplete, and that he, Paul, presumes to make up for the shortcoming? And does that not contradict what Paul had said almost immediately before in the same Letter: "It pleased God to make absolute fullness reside in him, and by means of him, to reconcile everything in his person, both on earth and in the heavens, making peace through the blood of his cross" (Col. 1:19–20)?

In the course of Christian history, in both East and West, there has been no consensus of what Paul meant here by "filling up what is lacking in the sufferings of Christ." Yet the passage has continued to intrigue Christians through the centuries, especially those who feel the gnawing ache of suffering in their bodies and minds. For as that suffering perdures through longer and longer periods, there is a feeling that, however complete the redemptive suffering of Jesus may have been, somehow it is not reaching their situation with its completeness and fullness. Something is lacking, something is not going far enough, for redemption and liberation are still not at hand.

This chapter explores this dimension of suffering in more detail. It touches on how we might understand solidarity in suffering— not only conforming our suffering to the pattern of Christ's death (Ph. 3:10), but also accepting the cup of suffering for the sake of others (Mk. 10:38). This exploration will begin by examining some of the ways this passage has been interpreted in Christian history, and then turn to the way it illumines a spirituality of the blood of Christ.

A Conflict of Meanings

Among the various interpretations of this verse over the centuries, there are some aspects of interpretation that meet nearly universal agreement. Most important of those agreements is that when Paul talks about the sufferings of Christ, he is not talking about the sufferings by which Christ expiated sin. With the exception of a very few contemporary Western exegetes, no one has ever claimed that Paul thought the sufferings of Christ for our sins were less than complete. That is to say, what has traditionally been called "objective redemption" (the basic liberation from a sinful state, which makes personal redemption possible) is not at issue in this Pauline passage.

It is interesting to note that there is no evidence of doubting objective redemption in Christ at all for at least the first twelve centuries of church history. The first explicit question about that possibility—whether Paul might be talking about some lack in the redemptive sufferings of Christ—is in Thomas Aquinas, and Thomas answers it in the negative. It was probably under the pressure of looking at salvation as expiation, and especially in terms of understanding salvation as a treasury of merits, that this question was first raised at all.

This position is further strengthened by the fact that Paul uses different vocabulary here for suffering *(thlipsis)* than elsewhere when he talks of the expiatory sufferings of Christ *(pathemata)*. Paul seems rather clearly to have something else in mind in this passage than the expiatory sufferings of Jesus. What might that be?

It is at this point that the interpretive tradition begins to fracture into a variety of possibilities. Basically, there are five major positions that have gained some credence in the course of the centuries:

1. One major interpretation goes along the following lines: when Paul says that he, in his own body, is making up what is lacking in the sufferings of Christ, he is engaging in what some exegetes have called Paul's "Christ-mysticism." That is, Paul is speaking of an experience of a mystical union with Christ. Perhaps the most famous example of this kind of Christ-mysticism, which some exegetes see scattered throughout Paul's writings, would be found in Galatians 2:19–20: "I have been crucified with Christ, and the life I live now is not my own; Christ is living in me." Now no one would say that Paul is speaking here about a literal crucifixion of his own body; he is trying to express an experience of union with the crucified Christ in spirit, a union that gives him a sense that now the crucified Christ is the very source of his own life. This exegetical opinion, therefore, would hold that Colossians 1:24 should be read as another example of this Christ-mysticism, wherein Paul identifies his own sufferings with those of the crucified Christ. The interpretation of the passage, then, would emphasize the solidarity of Paul's sufferings with the sufferings of Christ.

2. A second interpretation finds the key to understanding this passage in the final words of the verse: "for the sake of his body, the church." In this reading of the passage, Paul is referring back to his earlier metaphor of the church as the living body of Christ today, with Christ as its head (1 Co. 12:27). The parallelism of Paul's suffering in his own body, for the sake of making up what is lacking in the sufferings of Christ's body, is illumined by taking this approach. In this understanding, then, Paul is suffering on behalf of the church, which he is addressing. His suffering is tied to the work of perfecting of the members of Christ's body in the fullness of the grace of Christ. Paul's sufferings are redemptive of the community in a fashion analogous to those of Christ's.

3. A third interpretation is very similar to the foregoing one, but adds an additional dimension. It is found especially in the writings of St. Augustine, and was influential in discussions on the treasury of merit of Christ's redemption among medieval theologians. Like the second interpretation, this interpretation holds that Paul is talking about the sufferings of the members of Christ's body, which is the church. The additional dimension here concentrates on the nature of those sufferings. Augustine suggested that each member of Christ's body—each believer, therefore—is allotted a certain measure of suffering to endure. This brings a special element into the solidarity of the suffering of believers with the redemptive sufferings of Christ. Just as a cup of suffering was allotted to Jesus, so too are we allotted a measure of suffering. Our suffering is conjoined to the suffering of Christ as a way of bringing about the totality of redemption. If it is Christ who made it possible that suffering could be redemptive at all and not simply destructive, our redemptive suffering builds upon that foundation to help bring about the fullness of life in Christ. Given this vision of how redemption works, Paul would be understood to be talking here about his personal measure of suffering.

4. A fourth interpretation takes another tack. This position would hold that Paul really is talking about the sufferings of Christ. But at stake here are not the saving sufferings of the passion and death of Christ, but the sufferings that Jesus endured during his preaching and ministry in trying to establish the reign of God and the herald of that reign, the Church. Because the reign of God has not yet been fully realized, nor have all been gathered into the church of Christ, the ministry Jesus inaugurated is not complete— these works are not finished. Colossians 1:24 falls within a discussion of Paul's own ministry. Given that fact, the interpretation of

filling up the sufferings of Christ would mean that Paul sees himself continuing and indeed working to help complete one area of Jesus' earthly mission—namely, the preaching of the good news and the building up of the church. Just as Jesus struggled and suffered in his earthly ministry, so now does Paul. What is "lacking" in Christ's sufferings is what remains to be done in the preaching of the gospel and the establishment of the church.

5. A fifth and final position is similar to the preceding one, but adds a special dimension by focusing upon one element. The interpretation begins in the same way as the previous one, talking about the sufferings of the earthly Jesus in building up the reign of God and its herald, the church. The special focus then appears: Paul is singling out how his own sufferings fill up what is lacking in the process of announcing the reign of God and of building up the church because Paul is an apostle. As an apostle, as one sent in a special way by Christ, the sufferings in his ministry have a special character and value inasmuch as they closely imitate the sufferings in the ministry of Christ. Paul, so to speak, is acting in the place of Christ for the sake of the church, and so participates more closely in the sufferings of Christ than do ordinary believers. His suffering takes on special meaning and value for the church. Emphasis is placed here on the words "for the sake of." Paul suffers for the sake of the church, just as Christ suffered for the sake of us all. Because of the special relationship to Christ that Paul enjoys as an apostle, Paul's sufferings have a special value for the church beyond that of the suffering of other believers. They "fill up" what is still lacking in the sufferings of Christ in a special way.

Although other suggestions have been made in the course of Christian history for interpreting this passage, most commentators find themselves returning to one or other of these five positions, or to developing some combination of them. What is clear, however, is that there has been no consensus about the meaning of this passage, even among commentators of the same confessional tradition. What are the contemporary prospects for understanding Colossians 1:24, and how might that understanding illumine a spirituality of the blood of Christ?

If we assume that recent commentaries on this passage would represent opinions most attuned to the contemporary situation, it would seem that two of the positions discussed above find little following in the exegetical literature.

The first position, which holds that Paul is speaking out of a Christ-mysticism, is not much in evidence in the literature today.

This is no doubt influenced by the fact that Christ-mysticism is not a very clear concept, based as it is on scattered passages within the Pauline corpus, and is also not all that helpful in understanding other Pauline texts. This does not automatically rule out this position, of course. Such a Christ-mysticism can be found in abundance in Christian mystical literature, especially Western medieval literature about the blood of Christ. But when facing questions of suffering in the contemporary situation, it seems to be too removed from the concrete context of oppression and injustice, and too individual in its conceptualization to be helpful in situations where solidarity is of the utmost importance.

Likewise, the third position does not find many adherents among contemporary commentators. This position, growing out of Augustine's thought, sees each member of the body of Christ as being allotted some measure of suffering. Two things have militated against the acceptance of this position. On the one hand, it has more to do with Augustine's theology than with Paul's. That in itself is not sufficient to abandon the position. But a second factor makes searching for other possibilities more compelling. With the move away from scholastic models of speaking of redemption in terms of a treasury of merits, both among theologians and among believers in general, this kind of quantitative allotment loses much of its allure. This theology was the backbone of nineteenth-century spirituality of the blood of Christ (almost always spoken of with the economic attributive "precious" or "most precious"), which saw this spirituality as one of applying the merits from this treasury to the needs of the world, especially through the sacraments and good works. To a considerable extent, this model, with its economic and accounting metaphors, has slipped out of the awareness of most Christians today. Not that it was wrong; simply, it does not fit well with the other major dimensions that make up contemporary experiences of God's activity in Christ.

Positions two, four, and five all have some measure of following in commentaries today. These cut across confessional lines, so that one cannot speak of a distinctively Catholic or distinctively Protestant position.

For the sake of developing a spirituality that responds to contemporary situations of human suffering, two of these positions will be explored in more detail: the second and the fourth. Viewed from one perspective, they could be seen as being somewhat complementary or mutually supportive: suffering for the sake of the members of Christ's body, and suffering with the head of the body for the body's sake. Let us look at each of these and see what implications they might offer us for a spirituality dealing with suffering, and a spirituality of the blood of Christ.

Suffering with the Members of Christ's Body

The starting point of this position is baptism. In baptism, we are incorporated into Christ's death (Rm. 6:3), the full reality of his saving mystery. But by putting on Christ, we are gathered also by his resurrection into the new humanity (Ep. 4:24) and made a new creation. That new humanity, that new creation, is already coming about in the church, which Paul identifies as the living members of Christ's body. The sufferings those members now undergo because of their faith in Jesus Christ are indeed the sufferings of Christ.

This way of envisioning our relationship to Christ and understanding suffering becomes especially important when Christian witness leads to persecution, to the witness of blood. The sufferings of witnessing Christians take on a special meaning because they are conjoined with the sufferings of the head of the body. A special bond of solidarity is forged, drawing the sufferings of believers into the redemptive circle of the salvific sufferings of Christ.

Such a view of the sufferings of the just has implications for any spirituality dealing with suffering, and especially for a spirituality of the blood of Christ. For one of the most dangerous aspects of any kind of suffering is its capacity to isolate those who suffer from those who do not. If those who suffer are made to feel cut off and abandoned, there is a greater likelihood of a rapid disintegration of their sense of personhood.

One of the most terrifying things that can happen to victims of terminal illness, such as cancer, or to victims of mental breakdown is that, when they have been diagnosed as having a fatal or a mental illness, friends and relatives have a tendency to stay away from them, as though their illness were contagious. Often friends and relatives are not even aware of the deep fears that motivate them to act in this way. But if those who are ill are isolated from those who care for them, their prognosis for recovery is usually diminished. We all depend heavily on our relationships with others for our sense of identity and well-being.

When such relationships are deliberately cut off—as in the case of arrest, imprisonment, or exile—we are even more vulnerable to disintegration. It takes an extraordinary courage to sustain oneself under the duress of isolation in confinement. That is why solitary confinement is such an extreme form of torture. In these instances, those so imprisoned must know that they are not forgotten and firmly believe it if they hope to survive.

In any of these instances, there is a concern for forging bonds of solidarity in suffering. Solidarity in suffering does not mean that we experience exactly the same pain as those who suffer. If that were a precondition for solidarity, very little could ever be achieved. Solidarity does not reproduce the sufferings of others, but instead is a deep affirmation of their human dignity, even when it is threatened with disintegration by the onslaught of pain. My willingness to stay with those who suffer, even if that might mean a threat to my own well-being, is the foundation of the bond of solidarity. I stay even when it is not convenient, and even when it becomes dangerous. By so doing, I affirm that victims are more than the suffering they undergo, and that that suffering does not really define who sufferers are: sufferers are more than their illness, more than the degradation of their incarceration, more than the sum of their pain. That vigorous and relentless affirmation of human dignity is the basis for a rebonding of the human community and the further pursuit of new well-being.

But let us return for a moment especially to those who suffer for justice's sake, for the sake of their belief in who Christ is and what Christ has taught. No matter how they are called upon to suffer for Christ's sake, they need to know that their suffering builds up the living body of Christ today. Their suffering is conjoined with the suffering of Christ in a special way, and in so doing it opens up the saving reality of Christ to the members of his body in a way that cannot be achieved by other means. When that witness (what the Greeks called *martyria*) is to the point of blood, they unleash for the church a power by which the whole body of the church becomes stronger. "The blood of martyrs is the seed of the church," as Tertullian said long ago, and it continues to be true today. It has been estimated that the church has seen more martyrs in this century than in any previous period of history. And in those areas where the number of martyrs have been the greatest—in Latin America, in China, in the Philippines—the church is at its most vigorous.

Suffering drawn into the redemptive suffering of Christ can lead to the building up of the community of faith. The blood of martyrs, commingled with the blood of Christ, becomes the resource for resurrection, for new life beyond the violence and oppression of the present time. It is a pledge for vindication of those now locked in suffering. A spirituality of the blood of Christ becomes, then, a powerful resource for resisting oppression and coming to terms with the suffering that befalls communities and individuals. It takes away the isolative dimension of suffering and opens the way for a participative structure of solidarity, a process to affirm what Jesus himself affirmed by his willingness to die for our sake: the basic dignity of creatures created in the very image of God. The weakness manifested in suffering becomes a source of new life: "weakness is sown, strength rises up" (1 Co. 15:43).

Suffering with the Head of the Church

One of the interpretations above identified the sufferings of Christ that Paul speaks about in Colossians 1:24 with the sufferings of the earthly ministry of Jesus—namely, that Paul's own struggle to preach the gospel and to build up the church is in the same line with the struggles of Jesus in his own ministry. Read in this fashion, Colossians 1:24 becomes a juncture where a spirituality of suffering and a spirituality of ministry intersect. Jesus predicted that those who followed in the steps of his ministry would encounter resistance (Mk. 13:9), just as his own ministry ultimately led to his death.

Knowing that the furthering of the reign of God will lead to resistance from those who oppose it, Colossians 1:24, which binds together the suffering of those who minister with the sufferings of Christ—indeed makes them an extension of those sufferings into areas where Christ's suffering has not reached—offers a way to deal with the setbacks, the disappointments, and the struggles that inevitably come to those in the ministry of Christ. All these adversities are part and parcel of the completion of Christ's task to bring the gospel to every creature, and to allow the church to take root in every place and circumstance. In that building up of the reign of God through suffering (interestingly, medieval and baroque theologies referred to these sufferings of Christ as his "edificatory [i.e., constructional] sufferings"), the work of forging community and covenant is marked by the cross with all that it entails: disappointment, vulnerability, struggle.

Christ's shedding of his blood on the cross marked the end of his earthly ministry. It represented an endpoint beyond which he could not go in his preaching and healing activity. But it also came to represent a beginning: a redemptive act that would make the suffering of those who followed after Christ healing and redemptive as well. Suffering no longer meant certain destruction; another side was revealed. And in the struggle for justice in an unjust world, in the proclamation of good news where only bad news is being heard, the suffering Christ invites us to conform our suffering to his own. Our discipleship in ministry is not forgotten, even when those around us may not acknowledge it.

Conclusion

Colossians 1:24, enigmatic though it remains, has considerable power to offer to a spirituality of suffering, and to a spirituality of the blood of Christ. Basically, it helps establish how we, in our suffering, can participate in the ministry and saving activity of Christ. It gives meaning to struggle for solidarity in suffering. And it provides consolation and comfort for desolate moments in ministry. In this way, it is different from other elements of a spirituality of the blood of Christ, which might emphasize instead how we are recipients of God's great love. That is by no means denied here. Rather, Colossians 1:24 invites us to participate more directly in that saving activity. And living in a world where injustice calls Christians to be participants in struggle rather than distant observers, in a world where suffering and pain threaten to isolate individuals and communities, such an invitation to participation is deeply needed. And when the suffering we have freely assumed in solidarity begins to dim our own sensibilities, we can turn to the one whose suffering makes ours redemptive and know that what we do in that solidarity is not playacting. It is completing what has been begun in the sufferings of Christ.

In Water and in Blood

10

Jesus Christ it is who came through water and blood,
not in water only, but in water and in blood.
It is the Spirit who testifies to this,
and the Spirit is truth.
Thus there are three that testify,
the Spirit, the water, and the blood—
and these three are of one accord. (1 Jn. 5:6–8)

References to blood are not all that common in the Gospel of John and in the Letters of John. They appear in only three places in the Gospel: in the Prologue, in the eucharistic discourse of chapter 6, and in the description of the death of Jesus on the cross. In the Letters, there are but two places where blood is mentioned, both in the First Letter of John.

It is important to explore these few references, first of all, because of the importance of the Johannine writings in Christian history. These parts of the Christian scriptures have been especially prized. The writings of John, along with those of Paul, have been the most influential historically in shaping our understanding of Jesus and Jesus' relationship to God. Secondly, the references, although few in number, all seem to be quite carefully chosen and positioned in these texts by the author, and thus carry a great deal more weight in conveying the message of the Gospel and the Letters than might at first be imagined.

In fact, when these instances within the Johannine corpus are considered together, they represent a kind of summation of the major themes found within the Christian scriptures about the meaning of the blood of Christ. It is especially for that reason that they deserve our attention here. And so they will be explored one by one, first the texts from the Gospel and then the texts from the

First Letter, as a way of drawing together much of what has been said about a spirituality of the blood of Christ up to this point.

Not Begotten by Blood (Jn. 1:13)

The first reference to blood in the Gospel of John comes in the Prologue, which serves as a kind of overture to the rest of the Gospel. Toward the end of the Prologue, the author describes those who have become children of God: "These are they who believe in his name—who were begotten not by blood, nor by carnal desire, nor by man's willing it, but by God" (Jn. 1:12–13).

The reference to blood here is unusual, for in the Greek text the word "blood" is actually in the plural (*ex haimaton*), though it is usually translated in the singular (as in the *New American Bible* translation here). The meaning probably intended here is based on the understanding at that time of how children were begotten: by a mixing of the blood of the mother with the blood (semen) of the father. Thus all humans are born "of bloods." In this context the life-giving quality of blood is stressed. The life-substance of an individual was in the blood, and it took this commingling of life-substances to create a new human being.

A superficial reading of this text in the Prologue might at first convey the impression that the author is being rather negative about how the human condition comes about and is propagated. It is not by any human agency (by blood), any human desire (by carnal desire), or any other human striving (by willing it), that we become children of God. Rather, it is only through God's desire and action that this kinship with God can come about. A little later on, in Jesus' conversation with Nicodemus (3:1–21), the same need to be born again "from above" (3:3, 7) and "of the Spirit" (3:8) is emphatically stated. Moreover, the perduring contrast between flesh and spirit through this Gospel would also seem to play down or minimize the importance of human physiological generation.

To be sure, John's Gospel has often been read in this fashion. But one must remember that those who follow Jesus are also expected to eat his body and drink his blood, as real food and drink (6:54–55). Indeed only by such eating and drinking does one come to eternal life. In that famous discourse in chapter 6 (to which I will turn shortly) the body and blood of Jesus become the very vehicles by which we earthbound creatures come into the world of the divine, the world of everlasting life.

What is the significance of the reference to blood in this passage? It would seem that what the author of the Gospel is trying to do is paint the first part of a more complex picture. Throughout the Gospel of John there is an interplay between struggling to transcend the finite and death-doomed character of human existence, symbolized especially in the ultimate decay of the flesh, and the need to remind readers of the Gospel that Jesus was indeed flesh and blood, truly one of us, not some phantasm. The latter point is particularly clear in the account of the appearances after the resurrection: Jesus allows the disciples to touch his body (Jn. 20:27), he cooks fish and eats with them (Jn. 21:12–14). Jesus is at pains to reaffirm his physical presence, even though it is clear at the same time that he has been transformed and is now part of the world of everlasting life.

John's Gospel is a long meditation on the relationship between flesh and spirit. Flesh left to itself does not come to completion. Even blood, as the nucleus of the life of God within us, cannot of itself bring us into that transcendent reality that would mean our overcoming of death and decay. Left to ourselves, and in spite of our best efforts, we decline and finally die.

But the answer is not an utter abandonment of the flesh in a quest for the spirit. For we are indeed of flesh and blood, and cannot deny our nature. This comes out clearly in the Gospel's portrayal of Jesus. Even though the discourses of Jesus in John's Gospel are of a more spiritual nature, perhaps, than those of the other Gospels, there are many touching sketches of Jesus as profoundly human. One thinks of his getting impatient with his mother at Cana (2:4), or his being overcome with emotion at the tomb of his friend Lazarus (11:33).

The answer to the question about the relationship of the life of the flesh to the life of the spirit does not lie in separating them, but rather in some deeper, more profound relationship between the two. Somehow the true meaning of our earthly existence can be comprehended and illumined only through the power of the spirit. And the power of the spirit seems to lack form for us if it does not take on flesh and dwell among us (1:14). We are mixed beings, so to speak, both angel and ashes. That does not make human life inferior; rather, it opens up new possibilities for understanding the mystery of the life coming from God. Were human life simply inferior, it could be left to its own ultimate demise. But the Gospel of John is quite clear that this is not the case. In no other Gospel does Jesus speak so much of his mission, a mission not simply his own, but one coming directly from God. The affirmation of Thomas upon seeing the risen Lord (20:28) points to the culmination of that interaction between the world of this earth and the world of the divine: Jesus, born human, is the fullness of the revelation of the divine in our world.

Where does blood fit into all this? John 1:13 affirms the concreteness of human life by pointing to our human origins in desire and the mingling of bloods. As was noted above, this is the first part of a larger picture. The emphasis here is on concreteness: a concreteness to be transformed spiritually, but a concreteness nonetheless. It remains the fundament upon which the spiritual builds and in which the spiritual operates. It gives substance to the meaning of the eucharist as food and drink.

What this certainly emphasizes for any spirituality of the blood of Christ is that such a spirituality has to be involved intimately in the concreteness of daily life. It cannot remove itself to some spiritual height and speak in broad generalizations about the need for redemption in the human condition. In the image of the Gospel of John, we are born of the mingling of bloods; we are not born as an idea.

A spirituality of the blood of Christ seeks redemption for the human family in all its concreteness and all its fullness: in the alleviation of physical hunger, in the release from political and social oppression, in the relief from the anguish of the human heart. Such a spirituality, drawing especially from the Johannine vision here, realizes how much the elevation of the spirit depends upon affirming and attending to the physical and social reality of human beings. That is perhaps why the themes of bonding (covenant) and suffering (the cross) figure so prominently in this spirituality: a spirituality of blood does not begin with a theological concept and deduce its way down into human realities. It begins with something as concrete as our own physiological beginnings: born of blood. It recognizes that we cannot stay with those beginnings; but it realizes also that we can never really abandon them. A spirituality of blood is a spirituality of engagement with flesh and blood, an engagement that will allow the spirit to appear.

Flesh and Blood for Life Eternal (Jn. 6:25–71)

The long discourse in John 6 following the multiplication of loaves has Jesus presenting himself as the bread of life, the bread come down from heaven. This bread has a greater saving quality than did the manna eaten in the desert (6:49), for those who ate the manna died. Jesus makes the bold claim that those who feed on his flesh and drink his blood will not die, but will have eternal life.

What is so striking is the explicit way in which Jesus insists that those who seek eternal life must be willing to feed on his flesh and drink his blood. Such language taken literally would be naturally abhorrent, as the response of some of Jesus' audience indicates (6:52, 60–61, 66). The idea of eating human flesh was unthinkable, and the drinking of blood was sacrilegious. Why such astonishing language from Jesus?

Commentators point out that this passage can be understood only within the context of Jesus' passion and death. By urging his disciples to eat his flesh, Jesus was equating himself with the sacrificial lamb, whose flesh would be eaten as part of completing the cycle of sacrificial communication with God. The idea that his flesh is "bread come down from heaven" (6:51) is a play both upon his hearers' complaint that they already had manna and did not need Jesus as bread (6:31) and that the flesh of the sacrificial lamb, inasmuch as it was part of sacrifice, came down from heaven.

The background for understanding this discourse is certainly the Last Supper, where Jesus proclaims the bread and wine to be his body and blood, and gives them to his disciples to eat and drink. When these two elements are brought together—Jesus as the new sacrificial lamb and Jesus' institution of the eucharist—it becomes clear why there is such an emphasis on never dying and on eternal life. By conjoining sacrifice and Jesus' death, the saving character of participation in the eucharist receives special emphasis.

Seen in this fashion, the eucharist becomes more than a memorial to remember Jesus; it becomes a participation in the saving mystery of his death, the saving pathway whereby he opened up the possibility of tasting divine life. It has been speculated that, at the time of the writing of John's Gospel, some Gnostic groups refused to participate in the celebration of the eucharist, finding references to bread and wine as the body and blood of Jesus to be crude and unspiritual. The Gospel's emphasis on such participation is no doubt a response to that group. But more importantly perhaps for us today, it reinforces that intimate relationship between flesh and spirit explored in the previous section. By weaving together the themes of the Passover sacrifice, the manna from heaven, and the death of Christ, this passage helps illumine the relationship between flesh and spirit. The eucharist becomes the mediating presence that holds the world of the flesh and the world of the spirit together. To accept it for what it is—the body and blood of the Lord—is to live with the struggle of bringing flesh and spirit together in our world today.

It has been pointed out that behind this discourse there may be a reference to Ezechiel 39:17, where the prophet invites the birds to come eat flesh and drink blood as a sign of the endtime. In other words, by eating the flesh and drinking the blood of the Lord, Christians anticipate the eschatological fullness of the reign of God. It is an act of hope, then, in a future where the struggles between spirit and flesh will be overcome and reconciliation in fullness and truth will take place.

What does this mean for a spirituality of the blood of Christ? As was noted in chapter 6 above, the eucharist has always been central to this spirituality. Often that centrality has taken on the form of venerating the very presence of the Lord in our midst, of adoring the blood by which we have been saved. This remains a legitimate response to the eucharist, but the message of this passage in John brings some additional dimensions to this spirituality. It is, first of all, a very explicit acknowledgment of the contradictions with which many persons live. Flesh and spirit are not experienced as being in harmony. Attempts to force human life into certain patterns and molds that stifle the presence of the spirit speak of anything but harmony between flesh and spirit. Political leaders who impose oppressive social and economic policies upon their constituencies to "protect" them are actually stifling basic human dignity and perverting the rights attendant upon the dignity of the human person. Males who decide "what is best" for females; dominant groups who decide "what is best" for minority groups (as in the case of Anglo versus black and Hispanic groups in the United States, or European versus Amerindian groups throughout the Americas) are testimony to this contradiction. The "hard sayings" (6:60) of the eucharistic discourse remind us, too, of how hard the world is, and how strenuously the earthbound world tries to supplant the world of the spirit.

Participation in the eucharist becomes a way of coming to terms with those contradictions. The eucharist, by embracing the contradictions of life ("How can he give us his flesh to eat?"), can also bring a liberation from them. What Jesus gives us is food for eternal life, the overcoming of the conflict between flesh and spirit, in a life where the flesh comes to its completion and the spirit can be fully manifest.

The eucharist is, secondly, also nurture. As we have seen throughout these considerations, salvation often takes on very concrete form. It can mean protection from a night of terror; it can mean the vindication of a just cause and an ending of wrath, an invitation to draw near, the breaking down of separating walls, the chance to start over again. The prime image of the eucharist here is one of the most basic human needs: something to eat and drink. This need is not met in much of the world today, as the poor cry out for something to quell their basic hungers.

The eucharist, as portrayed in this discourse, gives something to eat and drink, satisfying both physical and spiritual hunger. It is a concrete, tactile encounter with the living God. The concreteness with which the Catholic traditions of Christianity have always approached the eucharist has its roots in John 6. The eucharist has to do with all the hungers of human life, not just the more refined or spiritual ones. To engage in the eucharist is to live in hope. To receive the eucharist is to commit oneself to the same things for which the Lord has died: the end of sin, and the coming of God's justice.

Blood and Water Flowing Out (Jn. 19:34)

The reference to blood in John 19:34 is part of the story of the death of Jesus. The soldiers were breaking the legs of those who had been crucified. The reason for this was that, by so doing, the crucified could not push themselves upward to relieve the pressure on their diaphragms. They would then die by suffocation. "But when they came to Jesus and saw that he was already dead, they did not break his legs. One of the soldiers thrust a lance into his side, and immediately blood and water flowed out" (Jn. 19:33–34).

That blood and water might flow out of a body is in itself not particularly noteworthy or unusual. But the author draws special attention to it, noting that this was the testimony of an eyewitness. Although it would not have been unusual ordinarily, in this instance it has special significance.

The precise intention of the author here is not entirely clear, but there seem to be a number of plausible possibilities. The blood pouring out of the side of Christ would be a most graphic representation of the completion of the sacrificial activity, a sign of the redemption effected through his death. It was also a sign that Jesus truly died, an argument against the Docetic elements in the Johannine community who downplayed the physical and human nature of Christ.

The fact that the blood is said to flow out evokes the image of a fountain for drinking. Hence, there may be a eucharistic reference here.

The symbolism of the water, however, is more complex. It has been suggested that the lance opening the side of Jesus to allow water to flow forth is to be understood alongside the story of Moses' striking the rock with his staff, and water flowing forth for the people (Nb. 20:11). This would be corroborated by Jesus' remark in John 7:37–38, where Jesus invites whoever is thirsty to come drink from him from whom rivers of living water flow. Or, it may be a reference to Ezekiel 47:1–12, where the prophet sees a stream of water flowing from the temple, a stream enriching all living things. Given that the Gospel of John sees the cross as the throne of the exalted Christ, this, too, would be a plausible explanation. Finally, throughout the patristic period, the water flowing from the side of Christ was seen as the water of baptism, now made efficacious through the shedding of the blood of Christ.

Whatever the precise meaning of the author here, it is clear that special attention should be given to the meaning of this event. It has been pointed out that there may also be some significance to the fact that in John 19:34 blood and water are spoken of, whereas in 1 John 5:6 the reference is to water and blood. How much can be made of the positioning is hard to say. Whatever the significance, it is at any rate clear that both blood and water have considerable significance for the Gospel of John. One need only think of the references to living water in the story of the Samaritan women at the well (Jn. 4:7–30) as but one instance.

My interest here is not to come to a single interpretation of John 19:34 (for, as was noted, several interpretations seem to be legitimate), but to explore the meaning for a spirituality of the blood of Christ.

A first thing to note is how closely the Gospel of John relates both blood and water. Jesus invites those who believe in him to drink from him: to drink living water and to drink his blood. Both give refreshment and strength, both can give eternal life so that one will never thirst again. One aspect of a spirituality of the blood of Christ, then, is a seeking to give refreshment or respite from the pain and struggle of life, and a reaching out to eternal life. It is a spirituality that recognizes the need to retire from the fray from time to time, to address immediate needs as a way of keeping on track for the longer struggle to bring about the reign of God. But even as it seeks refreshment for the moment, it cannot forget the call to a world where persons will never thirst again. It cannot forget the mandate to help bring about the reign of God and its justice. So this spirituality fosters a sense of hospitality for the weary and the stranger, a sense of care and nurture for those tired and in need of refreshment. It does this not to foster escape from the difficult realities and struggles of our world, but in order to foster a return to those struggles with renewed purpose. This spirituality reminds us that we are flesh and blood, not angels.

Patristic and subsequent theological speculation saw in the blood and water flowing from the side of Christ the birth of the church. The blood and water are viewed here sacramentally as signs of eucharist and baptism, the two sacraments upon which the church is founded.

For a spirituality of the blood of Chirst, a second possibility is opened up with this thought. This spirituality, grounded as it is in the saving activity of Christ, would see itself as helping bring about the church and helping the church through its need for constant rebirth. A spirituality of the blood of Christ has to do with the building up of his body, the church. And just as the blood and the water were the source of the church, a spirituality of the blood of Christ brings with it an awareness of to what extent and how often we must return to that birthing process: the church needs to return to its source and experience rebirth so as to remain faithful to its founder and to the gospel it preaches. A spirituality of blood, as has long been recognized in its history, is a spirituality of such renewal. It has its source of renewal in the blood and water flowing from the side of Christ.

Finally, the fact that the Gospel of John has blood and water—in that order—flowing from the side of Christ offers yet another possibility for this spirituality. It was through the flowing of blood—an act of dying, therefore—that the living water was able to come forth. In some ways, this is a paradigm for the death-resurrection process seen as so central to understanding God's saving activity in Christ. A spirituality of the blood of Christ, therefore, must recognize that before living waters can flow, before Ezechiel's vision of the temple as a source of life can be realized, death must take place. Struggles for a better world, hope for the resolution of seemingly irreconcilable differences, will probably come about only through death, the redeeming death of a life freely given in love for the sake of a better future. Often the death of victims of repressive political situations can be understood only in this way, for no other interpretation can make adequate sense of the evil and violence wreaked upon a community. This spirituality is a spirituality of martyrdom, one with ancient roots in the church, and unfortunately all too necessary still today.

The Blood that Cleanses Us from All Sin (1 Jn. 1:7)

This brief reference to the blood of Jesus comes within the context of the author's struggle against certain Gnostic teachers in the community who were always ready to speak of God as light, and to see themselves as walking in that light. The author of 1 John, however, notes two things here. First of all, if one claims to have fellowship with light, but continues in sinful ways, one is really walking in darkness. And secondly, that we can walk in the light at all is because "the blood of his Son Jesus cleanses us from all sin."

Two things are notable about the reference to the blood of Jesus here. First, the reference to the blood of Jesus as the means whereby we are brought into the communion of light is intended as a reaction against the intellectualizing tendencies of the Gnostic teachers. Once again, this passage in the Johannine literature is an instance of the effort to understand the relationship of flesh and spirit. Here something of the flesh redeems the spirit. This is underscored even further by the use of the verb "cleanse": a most physical, sensory process marks the act of redemption. Secondly, the verb is in the present tense. It is not just a historical event, but a continuing process that allows us to share in the communion of light.

This passage can be seen as a further filling out of the picture begun in the Prologue of John's Gospel. How the physical mediates the spiritual is brought forward here. Blood cleanses us from all sin. The use of concrete language ("cleansing" instead of, say, "transforming") underscores it. This provides a further insight into the relationship of spirit and flesh. The flesh—in this instance, blood—can provide entry into the world of the spirit where sin and its effects can be overcome.

For a spirituality of the blood of Christ, this helps us understand better the interplay between flesh and spirit. Again, as was noted above, the physicality of the blood as a vehicle for breaking through to the world of the divine life reminds us how concrete and physical is the forum for the struggle for liberation and justice today. It is not generalized; we often experience it as being all too specific. But 1 John 1:7 reminds us that the blood of Christ does not stand for us simply as a symbol of past achievements. It continues to cleanse from sin. It is present to us wherever Christ is present to us—in filling up what is lacking in the sufferings of Christ (Col. 1:24), in the Eucharist—wherever the presence of Christ is experienced. It is a living and moving force within our world, at the frontier where the reign of God is beginning to take shape. It heightens our awareness of both light and darkness, and offers us comfort and hope. This keen sense of presence gives a particular texture to this spirituality, a sense of immediacy but also the grounds for a great hope.

In Water and in Blood (1 Jn. 5:6–8)

This final passage from the First Letter of John might be understood as a summation or completion of the Johannine understanding of the blood of Christ. Two important statements in this passage provide the point of departure for reflection here.

First of all, "Jesus Christ it is who came through water and blood—not in water only, but in water and in blood." Here the double entry of Christ into the drama of salvation is affirmed: not only through water (probably a reference here to his baptism by John), but also through blood (probably a reference to his death on the cross). It was via his baptism and his death that he entered into this reality in a special way. By emphasizing these two points the author is once again concerned about countering Docetic teaching, which would make of Jesus more of a ghostly figure, only seeming to walk across the human stage, not a genuine human being. But it also refers to two pivotal moments in his mission: the inauguration of his ministry at the Jordan, and the culmination of his ministry upon the cross. Significant, too, is that Jesus does not come to us as an idea, but through concrete mediation: by water and by blood.

The second statement is that the Spirit, the water, and the blood all testify to Jesus, and they are of one accord. What is happening here is a kind of convergence between the Spirit, the water, and the blood. It is as though the author is recognizing that the reason for the significance of the water and the blood is that they both are vehicles of the Spirit. What gives the water its life-creating force, and what makes the blood procreative and redemptive, is the presence of the Spirit. Their testimony as to who Jesus is converges to give witness to the truth.

What does this mean for a spirituality of the blood of Christ? In some ways, to think of this spirituality as a spirituality of one who comes in water and in blood provides a focus for all the different aspects of the spirituality explored up to this point. The aspect of water emphasizes the life-giving side of the spirituality of the blood of Christ. It evokes the memory of the new life given in the waters of baptism, the life-giving water of John 4, and a host of contemporary understandings of water: the need for water in the sprawling cities of the Third World, the struggle over water rights in many rural areas.

When paired with water, the violent, death-dealing dimensions of blood are allowed a certain prominence. Not just the destructive dimension, but also the redemptive dimension is intended here. Blood as the sign of family bonding, and the fracturing of those bonds; the blood shed in injustice and filling the cup of God's wrath; the blood strong enough to cleanse from sin; the blood shed in the struggle for liberation in so many countries today; the blood of the innocent which receives no vindication—all these images, and more, flood into our consciousness here.

A spirituality of the one who comes in water and in blood is a spirituality that offers hospitality and a renewed life, and it also brings with it the prospect of witnessing even unto blood. It offers a cup of blessing and a cup of suffering. It is a spirituality that calls for solidarity with the poor and those who suffer, as close to concrete existence as the need for water and as essential to life as the flow of blood. To be a disciple of the one who has come in water and in blood is to attend to the physical and the immediate even as we hope for the future and struggle for a better world. It is to know the numbing ache of chronic pain and to experience the exhuberant rush of the dawning of our expectations. It seeks the healing of a fractured world and the rebirth of grace.

Conclusion

As noted at the beginning of this chapter, the references in the Johannine literature to the blood of Christ are few, but extremely suggestive for a spirituality of discipleship. Because of the dense texture of Johannine theology in the Gospel and in the Letters, these few references take on considerable significance. As this presentation has tried to show, they touch upon some of the most basic aspects of this spirituality and upon the experience of life itself: the relationship of this world and the world of God, the interplay of flesh and spirit, the meaning of the eucharist, and a spirituality that finds its way between immediate need and long-term struggle, between the need to refresh and the need to give witness even unto death. Thus, it is possible to see how the Johannine theology of the blood of Christ serves as a focus for the entire biblical understanding of the meaning of blood, and of the saving blood of Jesus Christ. In this way, it can serve as an adequate summing up of a contemporary spirituality built upon that biblical understanding.

11

Hope in Hopeless Situations

Brothers, since the blood of Jesus assures our entrance into the sanctu-
ary by the new and living path he has opened up for us through the veil
(the "veil" meaning his flesh), and since we have a great priest who is
over the house of God, let us draw near in utter sincerity and confidence,
our hearts sprinkled clean from the evil which lay on our conscience
and our bodies washed in pure water. Let us hold unswervingly to our
profession which gives us hope, for he who made the promise deserves
our trust. (Heb. 10:19–23)

In no book of the New Testament is the word "blood" mentioned
more often than in the Letter to the Hebrews. Yet those who
hope to find in that frequency of appearance a ready key to a
spirituality of the blood of Christ will probably find themselves put
off, at least initially. For the world of the Letter to the Hebrews
seems far away and almost completely out of reach to most persons
today. The language of heavenly rituals and liturgies, the depiction
of a universe densely populated by angels and other spirits, the
appearance of mysterious figures like Melchizedek—all of this
seems to bespeak a distant era with a message unable to touch our
own.

Part of the problem with trying to interpret the Letter to the
Hebrews for our own time is that Hebrews gives us so little to go on
by way of situating it in its own context. First of all, technically it is
really not a letter: there is no salutation at the beginning, and it is
not clear to whom it is directed. It is much more of a sermon than a
letter. Secondly, despite the title it has been given, most commentators agree that it was not written to a Jewish-Christian congregation. The title "Hebrews" was given to this piece of literature
quite some time after it was written, probably because of all the
references to Jewish temple ritual in the heart of the letter. Because
all the admonitions in the text against falling away from Christian

faith are never followed by a reference to reverting to Judaism, it
has been inferred that its addressees were not converts from Judaism. And finally, we do not know who authored this letter. Some in
the early church thought that the author was Paul, but the style
and some of the content are not Pauline—although there are certain affinities suggesting that it came out of a Pauline circle.

Not having any of the regular points to anchor an interpretation
of the text—audience, location, author—has meant that a great
deal more is left to the interpreter in making sense out of the text
than is usually the case. Thus, the background of the interpreter
often ends up providing the context for Hebrews. And there is some
evidence of this in the history of the interpretation of this text.

Roman Catholic commentaries on this text, for example, have
often emphasized the high priesthood of Christ in the heart of the
letter (Heb. 5–10) and have linked it with the sacramental priesthood of the visible church, showing how ordained priesthood flows
from the high priesthood of Christ. How many priests have used
Hebrews 5:6 on the commemorative cards for their ordination:
"You are a priest forever, according to the order of Melchizedek"?

A good number of Protestant commentaries, on the other hand,
make precisely the opposite point: because we have had a great
high priest in Jesus Christ, who has offered sacrifice once and for
all (Heb. 7:27), there is no longer any need for priests and priestly
rituals (Heb. 7–8). One cannot but wonder whether such approaches to commenting on Hebrews—Catholic and Protestant—
are more a reflection of Reformation debates than of first-century
concerns.

So how might one best approach Hebrews, and how might its
resources be opened for a spirituality of the blood of Christ? As was
noted above, Hebrews seems to be a rich possibility. But we need to
find a way of approaching this alluring text.

What I propose to do is follow out one strand of interpretation of
the Letter to the Hebrews, based upon a possible reconstruction of
its original context. Although such a reconstruction is by no means
certain, it has considerable plausibility. Arguments for the reconstruction are based upon internal evidence in the text indicating
that it is closely related to the Letter to the Colossians. If this is
indeed the case, it may mean that Hebrews was directed to a
community near Colossae and may be addressing some of the same
problems that crop up in the Letter to the Colossians.

On the basis of that reconstruction, I will explore four themes in
Hebrews that relate to a spirituality of the blood of Christ. This

particular interpretation, it seems to me, opens up Hebrews in a new way and deepens a number of themes we have seen emerging in a spirituality of the blood of Christ.

A Beleaguered Community

As was just noted, exegetes have discerned a number of textual similarities between Colossians and Hebrews. For example, the hymn at the beginning of Colossians insists that Christ has primacy in everything (1:18), and the beginning of Hebrews shows how Christ is superior to everything, even the angels, and is intimate with God (1:3–2:8). There are a number of other such parallels, particularly concerned with situating Christ in terms of creation and of God.

Likewise, there are parallels in curious passages, such as Colossians 2:20–23 and Hebrews 9:10, both statements against dietary restrictions. And both letters are preoccupied with the worship of angels.

These similarities have led some exegetes to hypothesize that the community to which Hebrews was directed may have been in the same geographical area as Colossae—namely, in the Lycus valley in Asia Minor. In Colossians 4:13–16 Paul makes links between the community at Colossae and the community at Laodicea, urging each community to read the letter sent to the other. Exegetes Charles Anderson and Robert Jewett have been led to suggest that perhaps the letter sent to Laodicea mentioned in Colossians 4:16 is what we now call the Letter to the Hebrews, given the similarity of themes in the two texts.

Whether or not the destination of the Letter to the Hebrews can be pinpointed so exactly, parallels indicate that the two communities may have been facing similar problems. From what we know of Colossae, and from discussion in the Letter to the Hebrews, what might those issues have been?

The community that received the Letter to the Hebrews apparently was facing challenges to its belief, and was experiencing some harassment and maybe even persecution. The numerous references to keeping faith, the long excursus on the great ancestors in faith (Heb. 11:1–40), and the exhortation to endure the trials they are experiencing (Heb. 12:7–13) all point to a community that felt beleaguered. To understand why the community felt so besieged, something of the worldview of that time and place needs to be understood.

At that time on the eastern edge of the Mediterranean, there was a fairly widespread belief that the world was surrounded by a host of spiritual forces and beings standing between the world and God. These spiritual forces had different names. Paul refers to them as the "principalities and powers" (Ep. 1:21; Col. 2:10). In Hebrews, they are often referred to as the "aeons" (*aiones*). Some contemporary Bible translations obscure this in the name of intelligibility to moderns. The *New American Bible* translation renders the term in a number of ways (e.g., as "the universe" in Heb. 1:2). These spiritual forces were often personified, and were believed to have power over particular parts of the world for a given period of time (hence the origin of the word "eon" in modern European languages). To be able to come into communion with God, one had to move, so to speak, through layer upon layer of these aeons before coming to the throne of God. In order to pass through these aeons, one had to placate them by rendering them worship and by other specific ritual practices.

Alongside these aeons were other spiritual beings called "angels," which could be either benevolent or malevolent. They were not defined territorially, as were the aeons. Some of the angels served as mediators between humanity and God. Others were evil, and tried to draw humans into the clutches of darkness. The angels, too, were rendered worship, either to gain their favor (in the case of the good angels), or to keep them at a distance (in the case of the evil angels).

This densely populated spirit world may seem strange to persons living in a different part of the world and some two millennia later. For persons living in industrialized societies, the invisible world is far more sparsely populated. But to dismiss this first-century worldview of eastern Mediterranean peoples as hopelessly naive or outrageously phantasmagoric is to deprive ourselves of the message of Hebrews. If this worldview and the message of Hebrews are reflected upon together, something very close to our own experience of the human situation begins to emerge.

The peoples of the first-century eastern Mediterranean, with their complex spiritual geography of powers and beings, and their equally complex rituals for dealing with that spirit world, experienced their day-to-day existence as one of living in a world that was out of their control. The resources they could bring to determine and give direction to their own lives seemed feeble and unable to affect that world to any significant degree. They felt surrounded and even overwhelmed by forces swirling about them that controlled their destinies without any special regard for them as a people or as a community. Consequently, they engaged complex rituals to try to communicate with these forces more powerful than they, in the hopes of bettering their earthly lot, and eventually passing beyond the earth to a happiness they were never to experience in the here and now.

At first, such a view of the world might seem alien to our own experience, but a bit of reflection reveals that the experience in the Lycus valley is not that different from what many people experience today. For example, in First World and in some Third World countries, the threat of nuclear annihilation hangs over the hemisphere like some brooding aeon. It has become a force that exerts an almost autonomous power over us. Although nations holding nuclear weapons have tried to make themselves believe that they really control them, the spectre of an accidental firing of a nuclear weapon that would set off a global holocaust is always lurking around the edges of such a belief. The unending rounds of arms reduction talks appear to be quaint rituals that can appease this aeon a bit, reducing somewhat the threat (although enough nuclear strike force remains to kill the entire world population many times over), even as nations, like persons possessed by a demon, continue to manufacture more of these weapons. To speak of the nuclear arms race as an aeon threatening our world may not be outlandish. And the first-century personification of menacing forces then becomes more understandable. And we share with first-century folk the experience of living with something out of our control.

That same experience can be had in other spheres of contemporary life. When one sees the grinding poverty of so much of the world, one may ask: How can something so massive in its proportions ever be reversed? A capitalist economy, which can seem so benign in the northern hemisphere, looks distant, uncaring, and exploitive from a southern hemisphere perspective. It is as though it has a life of its own, demanding tribute in the form of external debt. The impoverished are deprived of a decent human existence by forces so distant that they cannot even communicate with them. In the state socialist systems of the world, it seems as though other aeons roam about, imposing rigid central planning that seems destined to rule out prospects for the betterment of life for a local people.

The presence of aeons can be felt in the political sphere as well. Persons living in an atmosphere of terrorism feel little control over their lives and feel helpless to change their circumstances. Those who suffer for a long time under a dictatorship can also come to feel the presence of aeons.

These same forces can be experienced on a local level as well. Why does natural disaster strike those who are least prepared to deal with it? What causes mental illness? Why do some persons always fail, no matter how hard they try?

When viewed from these perspectives, belief in aeons and angels becomes more understandable. Such a belief is an attempt to give personality to forces that affect the environment. By so doing, it becomes possible, at least in some way, to relate to them, to open up the possibility of at least some communication.

The message of the Letter to the Hebrews is that there is someone who transcends in power all the aeons and angels. That someone has come among the beleaguered people of this threatened world, participated in their suffering, and because of his divine power has opened up a path through the aeons and angels directly to the throne of God (Heb. 8:1; 10:19–20). The first section of Hebrews identifies this figure as the Son of God, Jesus Christ. Jesus is in every way superior to the angels (1:4, 6, 13), to Moses (3:3), indeed superior to all of creation. By his suffering and death, he has offered the perfect sacrifice to God, a sacrifice that ends all other acts of worship to intermediate beings. We are called upon to place our total faith in Jesus, and to turn away from worship of angels and placation of aeons. The blood of Jesus, offered in that heavenly sacrifice, has made Jesus our new, heavenly high priest, a high priest of great compassion for us, who is able to sympathize with our weakness (4:15), and who invites us to approach confidently the throne of grace "to receive mercy and favor and to find help in time of need" (4:16).

Although not a priest when he was alive among us (8:4), Jesus now stands before the throne of God in our behalf. If we can keep from wavering in faith, we will bypass the menacing aeons and intermediary angels to come into the city of the living God "to the assembly of the first-born enrolled in heaven, to God the judge of all, to the spirits of the just made perfect, to Jesus, the mediator of the new covenant, and to the sprinkled blood which speaks more eloquently than that of Abel" (12:23–24).

In the meantime, we experience the test, as a way of purifying our faith and of strengthening our resolve, much as Jesus himself was put to the test (12:1–13). But this is but a prelude to coming into the new Jerusalem.

Such is the exciting message of Hebrews: a call forth from the imprisonment in the world of the aeons to a freedom before the throne of grace, an escape from the powers of this age to the power of the living God. This reversal in earthly events has been brought about by the blood of Jesus, who effected the atonement that eliminates the powers of the aeons and the evil angels, and brings us into closeness with God.

To explore more closely what this means for a contemporary spirituality of the blood of Christ and how it might be understood in our world today, let us take a look at four themes in Hebrews that can open up this message for us:

1. Jesus' solidarity in our pilgrimage;
2. Christ the great high priest;
3. Christ crucified outside the gate;
4. solidarity and hope.

Jesus' Solidarity in Our Pilgrimage

In the 1950s, the German exegete Ernst Käsemann drew special attention to the pilgrimage theme in the Letter to the Hebrews, expressed especially clearly in 13:14: "For here we have no lasting city; we are seeking one which is to come." The theme of being on the move pervades the entire letter. Readers have often been dazzled by the depiction of the heavenly liturgy and have not as readily noticed the pilgrimage theme.

There are a number of dimensions to this theme in Hebrews. Christianity itself was known in the early days not by the name "Christianity," but simply as "the way" (*ho hodos*). This manner of speaking about the experience of discipleship implies movement. Indeed, following after Jesus was seen as being on the way, the way of life as opposed to the way of death (Didache 1:1). The sense of being on the way or on a path implied, too, that the movement had a sense of direction. For many early followers of Jesus, this way meant a way out of sin and the trials of this world, and movement into the reign of God. To think of salvation as being led out of one condition and into another was already part of the Jewish heritage, with its exodus theme. But in the other religious traditions of the eastern Mediterranean of the time, the way was also seen as leading from this world, through the aeons, to the center of divine power.

And the pilgrimage motif also implied a sense of dissatisfaction with the current state of affairs. The current state was something to be left behind, even though that decision meant undertaking the perilous prospects of life on the road. Pilgrimage implies the need for change, for coming to live with the realities of the world in a different fashion. It is a bold act, for it cries out in the most forceful way possible that the current state of things is not only not adequate, but is in need of fundamental change.

Hebrews invites its listeners to leave one way of life behind. The placation of spirits and the rendering of worship to aeons will not bring about the salvation it seems to promise. The message for us today is much the same: to accommodate ourselves to the realities of nuclear holocaust, to passively accept political and economic dictatorship, to make one's peace with racism—although all of these might seem to reduce conflict in our lives somewhat, they do not, in the final instance, bring the peace they promise. One has to move away from those aeons and follow a different pathway if true salvation is to be found.

Hebrews warns us that undertaking such a pilgrimage out of the present age—that is, no longer allowing the aeons of the present to define our worlds for us—brings with it a measure of suffering and trial. For the aeons of the present do not easily give up their hostages. The aeons keep us as their slaves (2:14–15). And it will take the work of one stronger than the powers of the age to rescue us from that captivity.

The first section of Hebrews goes to great pains to announce that the one greater than the powers that rule the age is none other than Jesus. And chapter 2 of Hebrews makes the point that Jesus' overcoming of those powers was a result of his close identification with us and our suffering, even to the point of death. Our salvation from the aeons is happening already through Jesus' very identification with us:

> Surely he did not come to help angels, but rather the children of Abraham; therefore he had to become like his brothers in every way, that he might be a merciful and faithful high priest on their behalf, to expiate the sins of the people. Since he was himself tested through what he suffered, he is able to help those who are tempted. (2:16–18)

And a little later on: "For we do not have a high priest who is unable to sympathize with our weakness, but one who was tempted in every way we are, yet never sinned" (4:15).

What are the implications of this message of Hebrews about pilgrimage and Jesus' solidarity with us for a spirituality of the blood of Christ? Pilgrimage is a response to the seemingly impossible situation created when we are not subjects of our own history. When the aeons, rather than inner freedom, define who we are, we need a powerful one to come to our aid and lead us out of our bondage, leaving behind our current condition. It may not entail physically leaving our current place; indeed, more often than not, such departure is not even possible. But spiritually we do leave, we do declare that those constricting powers no longer exercise their dominion over us. And this pilgrimage is no aimless wandering, but a pilgrimage led by God. It is not for nothing that Hebrews speaks in this section (3:7–4:13) of the exodus. For this is the prime model of all such pilgrimages out of bondage. It is in the process of this pilgrimage that a band of slaves is forged into a people. The very act of pilgrimage opens up as part of the saving reality in itself rather than merely the prelude to that moment.

Thus, even for persons seemingly trapped in their circumstances, the Letter to the Hebrews offers a spiritual exodus to a place of inner freedom from which to battle the aeons. Oppressed peoples have often found such havens in history. One thinks, for example, of the black church in America and in South Africa as providing such a place from which to battle the aeon of racism. Hebrews has this theme of exodus running through it, an exit out of bondage and into liberation.

And in that exodus we do not wander aimlessly, because Jesus Christ has gone before us, opening up a path for us (Heb. 10:20). Through his suffering and his death, he experiences all that we experience: temptation, suffering, weakness. Hebrews seems to imply that it is not just Jesus' death or his entering into the heavenly sanctuary that brings about our salvation, for his solidarity in suffering is also part of his redemptive activity. For only out of that solidarity in suffering and weakness does his death in any way connect up with our lives. He has walked alongside us, and in so doing he could truly come to represent us before God.

This starts to fill out more clearly the theme of solidarity touched upon earlier. Solidarity with those who suffer is not simply an act of charity to which we are motivated by Christian kindness, but a bonding with them. And this bonding not only gives them support, but becomes part of their redemptive process.

It encourages those who suffer to keep faith, and so is an intrinsic part of their liberation. Our accompanying them is a sign that their pilgrim wandering is not aimless, but along a path that others have trodden and others can recognize. And finally, the solidarity of joining those who suffer provides a way for them to join their suffering to the suffering of Christ and so make their suffering a source of hope and strength rather than simply a destructive power in their lives.

To say that salvation is begun in solidarity reminds us that we are not passive agents in God's redemptive process. We are not led out in pilgrimage like pawns in a game of the aeons. It takes our active faith for God's saving power to touch us genuinely and fully.

For those who follow the way of Jesus and who honor his shedding of blood, we find ourselves being called to "not grow despondent or abandon the struggle. In your fight against sin you have not yet resisted to the point of shedding blood" (Heb. 12:3–4). Yet we follow him who did resist evil to the shedding of blood. And in that is our strength.

Christic the Great High Priest

Central to the argument of the Letter to the Hebrews is that the great saving act of Christ has brought about atonement for all sin and shortcomings, and by its power supersedes all previous and intermediary rituals, including the rituals of the temple.

That great saving act is depicted as the ultimate sacrifice of the Day of Atonement, when Jesus enters the heavenly sanctuary "not with the blood of goats and calves, but with his own blood and achieved eternal redemption" (Heb. 9:12). The ritual of the Day of Atonement turns out to be but a foreshadowing of the great and eternal sacrifice of Christ, the new and eternal high priest. This heavenly sacrifice inaugurates a new covenant (9:15), which redefines the people of God and offers salvation to those who adhere to it.

That Christ would offer his own blood, rather than the blood of goats and calves, is the natural consequence of the solidarity in pilgrimage discussed in the previous section. His solidarity with those estranged by sin, caught in the fear of death, and enslaved by the aeons had to be total. Jesus' very nature would allow for nothing less than that. It is that totality of earthly solidarity that makes the heavenly offering so utterly saving and liberating for us. Under such circumstances of walking with those who suffer, how could a vicarious offering be made without weakening the bonds of solidarity?

A second feature that Hebrews stresses is that Christ's priesthood is of the order of Melchizedek, not of Aaronic derivation. What is exactly meant in Hebrews by the order of Melchizedek is not entirely clear. There is some evidence that the appearance of a priest of the order of Melchizedek (that is, outside the standard line of priests) was evidence of the messianic age. Melchizedek's priesthood did not derive from his lineage, but was something freely given by God. Hebrews is insistent on not aligning Jesus with the Levitic priesthood. Chapter eight puts it baldly: "If he were on earth he would not be a priest" (v. 4). The nonlineal nature of his priesthood emphasizes how radically new is what is taking place, something so new that it requires a reconception of all things. His authority, however, does not derive from newness, but from his direct designation by God to act in behalf of all humanity.

Such an act presses the point that the worship of angels and aeons must now pass away, and those who continue in that vein are only deceiving themselves. By speaking of this act as the fulfillment of the Levitic ritual, which is but a shadow of the heavenly one now performed by Christ (8:5), God's previous dispensation is taken up into a new and more perfect one.

The high priesthood of Christ, then, emphasizes two things: the new order it creates and the nonreligious origins of Jesus' priesthood. The first emphasizes the new reality to which the community in the Lycus valley (and all who read this letter) was being called. It is a saving reality worthy of our trust and our hope, which will set aside forever the enslaving aeons of the present time.

And the second point is in harmony with a thought of Paul: no earthly religious legitimation gives the death of Christ its saving power and significance. Rather, God has chosen to legitimate the faith of Christ directly by making the cross the new Holy of Holies. Blood shed in human, societal violence becomes the saving blood that brings together heaven and earth, cleanses sin, and establishes a new and everlasting covenant. It will redraw the map of where dwells the sacred in our world. For God has taken up dwelling among the poor, the rejected, and the broken.

For a spirituality of the blood of Christ, what this part of Hebrews shows us is the reason for seeking out solidarity with those who suffer. We come to see how Christ in his solidarity was able to become the entry into the house of God, the everlasting sanctuary for those who suffer. That entry, as Hebrews 10:20 puts it, was through the veil of his flesh. This solidarity in suffering is more than spiritual. It was a concrete participation in every aspect of our existence.

And Hebrews holds before us, once again, the image of the new covenant, a covenant meant to last forever. What was valid in previous covenants remains in force here, but also more comes into play. Those who follow the spirituality of blood, with "hearts sprinkled clean" (10:22), now must work to make that heavenly sanctuary present and visible in the world about them. Their own solidarity with those who suffer becomes a visible sign of the bond forged already in the heavenly sacrifice.

Christ Crucified outside the Gate

But all the talk of heavenly liturgies and eternal sanctuaries should not allow us to forget the realities under which we still live. Hebrews reminds us:

> The bodies of the animals whose blood is brought into the sanctuary by the high priest as a sin offering are burned outside the camp. Therefore Jesus died outside the gate, to sanctify the people by his own blood. Let us go to him outside the camp, bearing the insult which he bore. (13:11–13)

Hebrews has Christ identifying with the bodies of the animals that were burned outside the camp. To be placed outside the camp or outside the gates in such a community-oriented society meant more than a shunning or an exclusion. It was a denial of existence itself, the ultimate act of Jesus' being made a nonperson. Yet it was in accepting this ultimate degradation that the fullness of redemption could be achieved. As was noted in reading Paul, the cross becomes the new dwelling place of God, juxtaposed against the pretensions of the human city, which tries to create its own reality on its own terms. But what counts for strong and weak, for acceptable and rejected, in that city is not held so by God. Hebrews has the pilgrimage procession of Christians going out of that humanly defined city and gathering around the cross. "Through him let us continually offer God a sacrifice of praise, that is, the fruit of lips which acknowledge his name" (13:15).

This helps bring some clarity to those hopeless situations in which we can find ourselves. To hope for salvation only within the terms of our own resources is to fool ourselves. Salvation calls for pilgrimage, acknowledging that the current situation cannot be the frame of reference. Rather, we must go out of that city and seek a crucified Christ outside the gates.

Seen in this fashion, that new and everlasting covenant inaugurated in the heavenly liturgy is not simply a grand spectacle representing the culmination of the current age. It is sharply critical of the presence of sin in the world today, of injustices left unrighted. That a new covenant had to be inaugurated says something about the state of our participation in the previous covenant.

That heavenly liturgy cannot be understood from the sanctuaries of our temples, but only from the perspective of being outside the gate, standing at the foot of Jesus' cross. It is only from that vantage point that we can come to understand what that heavenly liturgy is trying to say.

Solidarity and Hope

The Letter to the Hebrews, then, is not so much about complex ritual, or even about the hosts of aeons and angels that crowd its opening pages. It is about the struggle of a beleaguered people threatened with a loss of confidence in the promise it had been given. The Letter to the Hebrews has to do with solidarity and hope. The passage at the head of this chapter captures the essence of that message: through the blood of Christ we are assured entry into that heavenly sanctuary. We have a great priest who mediates in our behalf, overcoming all the aeons that press in upon our existence today. We should, then, renew our confidence in him who deserves our trust, even as we struggle along on what sometimes seems an uncertain pilgrimage out of the world we know into the unknown, outside the gate. The Letter to the Hebrews is meant to remind, admonish, and encourage those who struggle with the aeons of this age and look forward to their own entry into the heavenly sanctuary. They know that the path of pilgrimage is fraught with temptation, suffering, and persecution, as it was for Jesus. But their future is guaranteed in the blood of Christ. They are already members of a new covenant sealed in his blood.

For those who follow a spirituality of the blood of Christ, the themes of solidarity and hope enunciated in Hebrews become central ways of expressing that spirituality. Solidarity in water and in blood, solidarity in walking the way of the cross, solidarity to the point of shedding blood is part of the life of those who follow this form of spirituality. But solidarity in aimless pilgrimage is only shared delusion. True solidarity is grounded in faith, the faith that is "confident assurance concerning what we hope for, and conviction about things we do not see" (Heb. 11:1). The blood that Christ has shed, the same blood offered in that heavenly sanctuary, is the source of that unshakable hope, which can sustain us when all about is very tenuous and uncertain.

The vision of the heavenly sanctuary sustains us even as the cross outside the gate calls us to commit ourselves to those to whom Christ has committed himself on this earthly pilgrimage.

Washed in the Blood of the Lamb

Then one of the elders asked me, "Who are these people all dressed in white? And where have they come from?" I said to him, "Sir, you should know better than I." He then told me, "These are the ones who have survived the great period of trial; they have washed their robes and made them white in the blood of the Lamb." (Rv. 7:13–14)

The Book of Revelation, that collection of apocalyptic visions filled with elaborate and illusive symbolism, stands at the end of the canon of the books of the New Testament. Its violence and often unbridled imagery caused some early Christians to want to exclude it from the canon of sacred books. But despite their efforts, it has remained part of the collection of the scriptures.

The character of Revelation has been disturbing to some, but for others it has been a source of consolation, especially for those caught in the grip of oppression and persecution. It has represented a hope for vindication from the onslaughts of evil experienced in the present time. Perhaps that it is one of the reasons why it was kept in the New Testament canon despite the opposition to it.

At the same time, the imagery of this book has been subject to exploitation. It has been used by some as a road map to the immediate future, rather than as the book of consolation and encouragement for the persecuted that it was probably intended to be. And in a few tragic cases, such as during the National Socialist period in Germany in the 1930s, it was used to bolster the proclamation of a thousand-year *Reich* (Rv. 20:4).

My interest here, however, is to see what this book might contribute to a spirituality of the blood of Christ. That it might have something to say to this spirituality is certainly suggested by the fact that it has been a popular source of preaching on the blood of

Christ in many churches, especially in the image of the blood of the lamb. The word "blood" appears some nineteen times in Revelation; only in the Letter to the Hebrews does it occur more frequently. And a closer examination of the text will turn up a complex and rich symbolism that offers some special perspectives on the blood of Christ, and also sums up many of the reflections that have been offered in the first part of this book.

The focus here will be upon understanding the meaning of the blood of the lamb, presented as a figure for Christ. Interestingly, there are only four other references to Christ as a lamb in the New Testament: two in the Gospel of John, and one each in the Acts of the Apostles and in the First Letter of Peter. Paul, in his rich reflections on the meaning of salvation, has no reference to the lamb at all.

But before coming to a discussion of the lamb, and the blood of the lamb, it might be helpful to give first some background to the Book of Revelation, and examine other uses of the concept of blood within this book. This will all form a helpful preparation for examining the meaning of this much-loved symbol in Christian tradition.

Background to the Book of Revelation

The Book of Revelation is presented as a series of visions of one John on the island of Patmos. In these visions, John is taken up into heaven and sees the future, which includes a great tribulation about to come upon the earth. It will be the final struggle between the powers of God and the forces of evil, forces now incarnated in the enemies of the Christian community. These enemies are already engaged in an active persecution of the Lord's elect. This struggle between the forces of good and evil will mark the end of the world in its current form. Because of that, the final struggle will be a terrible one, for the forces of evil are not weak, and they realize that this is the final battle. There will be no future for them if they lose.

The Book of Revelation is addressed to a people laid low by persecution; its members have suffered for so long that they are tempted to doubt whether they will receive relief from their travails at all. The book is written as a comfort to them. The seer John reports what will soon come to pass; they should therefore not lose hope or weaken in their faith. God is coming to vindicate them, and their oppressors will be swept away. The intensity of the closing verse of the book expresses the yearning of a people in pain and anguish: the Lord says, "Yes, I am coming soon!" To which the response is given, "Amen! Come Lord Jesus!" (22:20). One can feel the keen anticipation of the community of the believers in those poignant words.

Revelation often speaks in code, using symbols immediately recognizable to the persecuted community, but of obscure meaning to outsiders. This is not surprising, for a persecuted people or a group under occupation must often revert to such a tactic to preserve itself and communicate its message. The symbols used in Revelation are often rich in allusive references to other parts of the scriptures. They evoke whole passages of the Bible, especially passages speaking of God's dramatic interventions on behalf of a beleaguered people.

Exegetes are not agreed on just when this book was written, but the majority seem to favor dating it from the persecution of the Christians by Vespasian, toward the end of the first century.

Before turning directly to the theme of the blood of the lamb, let us first examine two other themes of blood in Revelation: the blood shed in violence, and the blood of the saints.

The Blood Shed in Violence

Not all the references to blood in the Book of Revelation are by any means related to the blood of Christ. In a number of places the negative or destructive side of the symbol of blood as a sign of death is used to represent the utter destruction about to be wreaked upon the earth. Thus, when the forces of God come to visit God's punishment upon a sinful earth, blood often appears.

For example, when the sixth seal is broken open on the scroll, "there was a violent earthquake; the sun turned black as a goat's-hair tentcloth and the moon grew red as blood" (Rv. 6:12). When the seven angels begin to blow their trumpets, "there came hail and then fire mixed with blood, which was hurled down on the earth," after which a third of the sea is turned into blood when a fiery mountain is plunged into the sea (8:7–8). When the seven angels begin to pour out the bowls of God's wrath upon the earth, "the sea turned to blood like that of a corpse" (16:3), and the rivers and springs turned to blood (16:4).

The blood in all of these images emphasizes the ominous side of blood symbolism. The blood presented here is the blood of violence, of struggle, and of unbridled wrath. The angel who has turned the rivers and springs into blood cries out: "To those who have shed the blood of saints and prophets, you have been given blood to drink" (16:6), a blood of wrath that has already killed every living thing in the waters. This blood of wrath is God's scathing protest against the oppression of the elect. It is a wrath that has been collected in bowls until the proper time for its being poured out upon the earth (15:7; 16:1). The message is clear: God's wrath against injustice does not pass with time. It remains as a painful memory, and has been preserved in order to be meted out upon evildoers in the final struggle. God does not forget the sufferings of the saints.

Now the point of the image is not to portray God as petty and vengeful. Rather, the pouring out of God's wrath and the vindication of the elect shows how seriously God takes every action in the world. Nothing is so trivial that it is forgotten. Moreover, God's vindication of the elect is a response to their fidelity to God. It is a seal upon their lives of fidelity to the covenant, for the sake of which God brings about the justice denied the elect in their lifetime. It is not that God takes delight in punishing; what it shows is how seriously God takes the pursuit of justice and how deeply God cares for those who are oppressed. What the image makes clear is that when God's vindication comes, it will literally shake the earth.

The Blood of the Saints

The blood of violence, the blood of God's blazing wrath, is not the only kind of blood spoken of in the Book of Revelation. As the reference to making evildoers drink the blood of wrath indicates, blood also refers to the blood of the martyrs, those witnesses to God who have been tortured and put to death for their belief. At one point, the seer John says:

> I saw under the altar the spirits of those who had been martyred because of the witness they bore to the word of God. They cried out at the top of their voices: "How long will it be, O Master, holy and

true, before you judge our cause and avenge our blood among the inhabitants of the earth?" (6:9–10)

At another point John sees the whore Babylon "drunk with the blood of God's holy ones and the blood of those martyred for their faith in Jesus" (17:6).

The blood that flows through the visions of the seer John is not only a symbol of God's all-consuming wrath, therefore, but also is the blood of God's holy ones. None of that blood will have been shed in vain. God does not forget those who have remained faithful, nor is the pain marked in their shedding of blood forgotten.

All these uses of blood were, of course, very important to the first readers of this book. The blood they shed now, the blood they see their loved ones called on to shed, is not shed in vain; nor will it be forgotten as it seeps away into the earth. Fidelity will be rewarded with vindication. The powers of evil, incarnate in those who oppress and persecute, will not be allowed to define ultimately what the world is like. God's justice will come to rule.

The Blood of the Lamb

In chapter 5, the seer John sees "a lamb standing, a lamb that had been slain" (5:6). The elders gathered around the lamb begin to sing:

> Worthy are you to receive the scroll
> and break open its seals,
> for you were slain.
> With your blood you purchased for God
> Those of every race and tongue,
> of every people and nation. (5:9)

Who is this mysterious lamb being so worshiped? The seer John leaves little doubt: it is Christ. But the Christ who is presented here is draped in a rich symbolism that evokes a range of different memories and themes.

The lamb here recalls the Passover lamb, whose blood gave protection to a slave people threatened with death in a foreign land (Ex. 12:3–13). The lamb in Revelation 5 has been slain, evoking the suffering servant of the Book of Isaiah, who was led as a lamb to slaughter (Is. 53:7). And the meaning given to the slaying of the lamb in the song of the elders evokes the blood rituals of the sacrificial lambs of Israel. But the lamb also evokes the memory of the innocent lamb—harmless, guileless, and vulnerable. The lamb in Revelation becomes a symbol both of those who suffer injustice and of their vindication.

The lamb in this vision has been slain. The word translated here as "slain" (*esphagmenon*) does not have a particularly ritual meaning. It refers rather to someone who has been brutally and ruthlessly cut down: a victim of violence. The image that this very secular word evokes is not one of sacrifice, where life is freely given up for the sake of holding the world together, or for reconciling hostile parties. The image is rather one of murder in all its profanity. This certainly evokes the memory of the very profane and violent death of Jesus, executed as a criminal on the cross. But this lamb, which had been slain, now stands. The lamb still clearly bears all the wounds of its slaughter, yet it is clearly alive. What this coded image would have meant to the persecuted community reading it is that the slaughtered lamb has been raised back to life: it is none other than the risen Christ.

But in the hymn, the point is made that despite the violent death of the lamb, the slain lamb's blood has redemptive powers. It has been a ransom to free an imprisoned people, and to create of it a new people for God, just as blood sealed the covenant and created a people in the Sinai wilderness (Ex. 24:8). It recalls, too, the symbolism of the blood-ransom in the letters of Paul and in the Letter to the Hebrews. This oscillation in the symbol between violent slaughter and redemptive creation of a new people tries to hold together the memory of the cruelty and viciousness that the saints had experienced in their own bodies, and a deeper level of meaning whereby these horrors are transformed into the redemptive gathering of broken victims into a new covenant. The death of Christ is seen as at once an execution in all its violence, and a sacrifice that restores the world and forges a new people.

It is difficult to hold these two views together. The standing-slain lamb, binary in its symbolism, seems to be the only image capable of conveying this moving experience. Christians who had seen their comrades executed for their faith had to deal with the horror of the event, and yet see within their deaths a deeper meaning: their deaths were somehow connected with the death of their executed leader, the Lord Jesus Christ. Thus the lamb, and the blood of the lamb, become the prism through which the meaning of their suffering and oppression can be understood.

Surely this powerful image from the vision of John continues to have meaning for oppressed peoples today. When people have to deal with the disappearance, imprisonment, torture, and death of their loved ones, the symbol of the lamb, slain but now standing, can provide a pathway through their anguish to a life-giving hope. When death squads appear in villages to kill at random, the lamb stands among those who have fallen. There are few places where the spirituality of the blood of Christ is more powerful than in such circumstances. For those grief-stricken persons can take comfort in the fact that Christ knows the wounds of their loved ones, that he has gathered to himself those who have fallen, and that they will follow him wherever he goes (Rv. 14:4–5).

Washed in the Blood of the Lamb

I turn finally to the vision of Revelation 7:9–17. In this passage, the seer John views a huge crowd of persons dressed in long white robes and praising the lamb. The elder standing next to him asks John two questions: Who are these people? Where do they come from? John defers to the elder and persuades him to answer his own question. He does so, saying: "These are the ones who have survived the great period of trial; they have washed their robes and made them white in the blood of the lamb" (Rv. 7:14).

The huge crowd, "from every nation and race, people and tongue" (7:9), are the same ones who have been made God's people through the blood of the lamb (Rv. 5:9). They have been oppressed and persecuted, even into death, but have "survived"—that is, not wavered in their faith. They have survived the trial, too, in the way an athlete survives a competition and trial of strength. Their own spirituality of struggle, their own prayer that led to blood (Lk. 22:44), has brought them to the triumph of the lamb. That they have washed their robes and made them white in the blood of the lamb is a deliberate use of contradiction in symbolism once again—for blood stains, it does not make white. But their garments are no longer stained, like the blood-stained garments of the lone warrior from Bozrah (Is. 63:3). Their washing them in the blood of the lamb has made them white, the color of the resurrection. The blood of the lamb, shed in violence, is also the blood that overcomes violence and death. As a medium of communication with God, it brings the just and redeeming God into contact with the unjust and oppressive world where the people of God has been put to death. It is the blood that purifies what has been profaned (Heb. 9:22)—in this case, the bodies of the saints. And so they now share in the bright, white light of the resurrection. The blood, as embodying the life-force of God, prevails over destruction and reestablishes life.

The image of the saints washing their robes in the blood of the lamb suggests that the blood has become a font of living water, welling up to continue to nourish and protect the saints. The notion of blood as life, so pervasive in the history of Israel, now reveals the fullness of its meaning. The font of life, the font flowing from the wounds of the lamb, purifies, protects, and nourishes the saints. Here the expiatory, redemptive, and eucharistic symbolism of blood converge in the figure of the life-giving lamb. The saints are purified of the indignities heaped upon them, they are protected from further harm by being drawn into the circle of a new covenant, and they are fed by the lamb.

The vision of the font here evokes the memory of another vision, that of Ezechiel 47:1–13, where the prophet saw the river of water flowing from the temple and turning the barren countryside into a paradise. And all of this brings into full evidence the meaning of God's new covenant, which overcomes all the destructive forces that have torn apart the fabric of the human community.

The symbolism is staggering in its power, for the range of meanings of the blood converge here as they do nowhere else in the scriptures. The blood that protects, overcomes death, purifies and sustains life is now fully manifest. And the full freight of that meaning can be appreciated especially by those who have felt the great trial in their own bodies. The lamb gives to a people whose bodies and world have been shattered a security that obliterates the horrors wreaked upon it. We know that victims of violence suffer aftershocks of terror for a long time after the event because that act of violence has shattered their basic sense of security. But the lamb has restored their sense of trust:

> Never again shall they know hunger or thirst, nor shall the sun or its heat beat down upon them, for the lamb on the throne shall shepherd them. He will lead them to springs of life-giving water, and God will wipe every tear from their eyes. (Rv. 7:16–17)

This is what a spirituality of the blood of Christ has to offer to victims of violence. The lamb, still bearing the wounds of violence upon its body, protects those who have been victims and leads them to life-giving water. And so for those who live by this spirituality, a powerful means of counteracting the effects of violence and terror is given. For when we hold up the blood of Christ, when we offer that cup of suffering and blessing, when we celebrate the covenant that holds the world together, we are giving a struggling people the very life-force of God, a life-force that contends with death in all the forms it assumes in our world. A spirituality that communicates this great gift of God to a troubled people can contribute much to the building up of the body of Christ and to creating a more just world.

Solidarity and hope in the blood of Christ: to walk with those who suffer and never forget the new covenant that is held out to us as a great hope. These are at the heart of the spirituality of the blood of Christ.

Epilogue

THE SPIRITUALITY OF THE BLOOD TODAY

This book has tried to explore some of the resources for a contemporary understanding of a spirituality of the blood of Christ. It has done so by means of twelve examinations of biblical texts and themes. By its very nature, such an exploration does not produce an analytical or tightly woven account of a spirituality; the result is a more open-textured work that unveils more possibilities than it explicitates. As was indicated in the Introduction, the intent was more to develop the biblical resources for reflection on a spirituality of the blood of Christ than to provide a definitive account of it.

Nonetheless, it may be of some use to try to draw out here some of the principal motifs that have appeared and order them in some fashion, so that individuals and communities can make the wealth of the biblical material on this theme more their own. To that end, this Epilogue does three things: (1) it begins with a brief description of what has been meant here by spirituality; (2) it returns to the two principal motifs of a spirituality of blood—expressed as community and conflict, or solidarity and hope; and (3) it explores those motifs through three biblical images that came especially to the fore—covenant, cross, and cup.

Spirituality Today

The term "spirituality" admits of many meanings and many uses today. In some instances, it is used to replace the older term "devotion"; in other instances, it means something closer to lifestyle. It is worthwhile to detail how it has been understood in this work and will be used in this Epilogue. There are four principal characteristics to its use here.

130

1. *Spirituality is the expression of the Christian meaning of our lives as individuals and in communities.* This is the broadest part of the understanding of spirituality at work here. It is our response when we are challenged to say what motivates our actions, directs our lives, and describes our relationship to God and one another as Christians. To that extent, spirituality needs to be explicit—that is, expressed in outward form and words, both for individuals and within communities.

2. *Spirituality is rooted in a distinctive understanding of the gospel of Jesus Christ.* This dimension of the understanding of spirituality recognizes that the gospel of Jesus Christ is so rich in its possibilities that individuals and communities must seek out pathways through that gospel, so as to live in a manner faithful both to the gospel and to their current situations. Not to do so can easily lead to an eclecticism that takes the challenge out of the gospel's "hard sayings" or allows one to ignore aspects of one's own circumstances. Following a distinctive understanding—while not excluding other insights from the gospel—allows one to build a focus and center in one's life and one's relationship to God. A spirituality of the blood of Christ is, of course, such a distinctive understanding—not the only one the Gospels yield, but certainly a very rich one.

3. *Spiritualities are concrete and express themselves more in images than in concepts.* As contrasted with theologies in the strict sense, spiritualities are concerned with the concrete tasks of daily living in a specific context. They are therefore concerned with more than the intellectual or cognitive, although they by no means exclude this dimension. They are concerned with concepts, but mainly as to how concepts are translated or applied to a specific problem or situation. For that reason, they are more often expressed in images or embodied in exemplary individuals than in conceptual categories. Thus, a good deal of space was given in this book to referring to concrete situations where a spirituality of the blood of Christ might be most effective in a given situation. And a great deal of time was devoted to unfolding the image of blood to reveal its capacity to hold together within itself a wide variety of concepts and meanings: life and death, community and conflict, redemption and reconciliation, solidarity and hope.

4. *Spirituality is rooted in both Christian tradition and contemporary experience.* Spiritualities have a dual rootage. They find their nourishment first of all in a tradition—in this instance, the Christian tradition. In this dimension they are intended to embody the collective experience and wisdom of those who have tried to follow

after Jesus. Thus, for a spirituality to call itself Christian, it must resonate with the larger Christian tradition. At the same time, however, a Christian spirituality needs to be rooted in contemporary human experience. Not to be so founded will lead to an antiquarianism or romanticism that will necessarily fall short of truly responding to the mission of the Christian in the world of today. Because of this double rootage, authentic Christian spirituality neither incorporates all contemporary experience into Christian tradition, nor does it accommodate the gospel to contemporary culture. It is instead a mutually critical and mutually correlative activity, whereby Christian tradition challenges the interpretation of our contemporary experience, and contemporary experience challenges the way we interpret Christian tradition.

The spirituality presented here has tried to exemplify these four characteristics. Explored were the many ways it can give shape to our lives as Christians and help to understand God's designs for the world. Its meaning in the life and message of Jesus was examined from different perspectives of biblical writers. The meaning of its imagery and the concepts that could explain dimensions of that imagery were pursued. And I highlighted how tradition makes us rethink our own understandings of a contemporary situation, and how contemporary experience makes us rethink customary interpretations of tradition. Let us turn now to some of the understandings that have emerged in that process.

Community and Conflict—Solidarity and Hope

As was noted over and over again, the ability of the symbol of blood to hold within itself meanings about both life and death is the source of its expressive power. It is that struggle about life and death that lies, of course, at the heart of the Christian message: salvation in God through the death and resurrection of Jesus Christ. Those meanings were explored in turn via a whole series of related ideas: community, safety, human rights, bonding, communication, communion, solidarity, blessing, hope, hospitality, justice, reconciliation, forgiveness, expiation, and vindication—as signs of life; and violence, struggle, chaos, isolation, wrath, oppression, injustice, suffering, conflict, sin, alienation, imprisonment, exile, and abandonment—as signs of death.

Two of these stand out especially as characterizing the task of those who follow such a spirituality and try to give concrete expression to it in their lives: community and conflict.

Blood as a sign of life and the bond that holds together families, tribes, peoples, and nations (Rv. 5:9) calls those who see the blood of Christ as a prime carrier of the gospel's meaning to work for the building up of community. They are keenly aware, too, to what extent community is under threat of disintegration from within and destruction from without. In cultures where individualism is the governing ethos, loneliness and isolation weaken the bonds of community. In oppressive situations, outside forces work to weaken the bonds of solidarity that give persons strength in the face of the dominating forces. The affirmation of these bonds, the cultivation of hospitality, the bringing near of those once far off, the promotion of forgiveness and reconciliation—all these stand as priorities in evangelical witness to the strength of the blood of Christ.

In cultures of abundance, this face of the spirituality of the blood of Christ is more in evidence and more in need. Perhaps this is because cultures of abundance can ignore or escape more of the conflicts of life thanks to their greater resources. At any rate, following a spirituality of the blood of Christ here leads one to commit oneself to the community-building process at all levels of society—families, neighborhoods, cities, and nations. It extends from healing broken families to a concern for peace among nations.

Conflict represents the other side of this spirituality. Generally speaking, we tend to avoid conflict if we can, be it conflict between individuals or social conflict. Yet a spirituality of the blood of Christ acknowledges the prevalence of conflict in the world, and realizes that conflict does not ebb when it is ignored. Conflict points always to the brokenness and sin in the world, to evil and injustice. A spirituality of the blood of Christ offers a way to prepare oneself for entering into conflict and staying there with those who struggle. It teaches the value of solidarity; it helps to discern true relationships of power and weakness; it provides mental and spiritual preparation; it gives a hope that reaches beyond the immediate situation; and it connects up current suffering with the suffering of Christ.

This dimension of spirituality is especially helpful to those who live in situations of conflict, and who commit themselves to being with the marginated in society—those who usually feel the conflicts and contradictions of a society most keenly. The cross of

Christ is the dwelling place of God for the lowly; redemption and liberation can be hoped for through the blood of that cross.

But even for those living in more comfortable situations, conflict is still part of life. It means not using a convenient escape to avoid problems at hand. It means, too, recognizing the contradictions and injustices that make one's own comfort possible. The blood of Christ calls out for the building of community, but also for the commitment to justice, a justice in which true peace and true community can come about.

Biblical Images: Covenant, Cross, and Cup

Another way of bringing together the main lines of a spirituality of the blood of Christ is to return to three other images that intersect with the theme of blood in the scriptures: covenant, cross, and cup.

Covenants were the signposts by which the chosen people marked its history with God. From Abraham and Sarah through Moses and David, bonding and rebonding gave expression to Israel's relationship to and experience of God, on the one hand, and to its own self-definition, on the other. And it was not surprising that Jesus would speak of the relationship he was forging between God and his disciples in terms of covenant.

Covenants in the history of Israel were sealed in blood, as was the covenant Jesus sealed with his disciples. A spirituality of blood is a spirituality of covenant, of healing the broken covenants that litter the landscapes of families and nations. A spirituality of covenant has to do with drawing into a circle of care those who are considered outsiders and nonpersons in a society. It has to do with reestablishing trust when confidence and respect have been trampled upon. It has to do with seeking reconciliation after war and the breakdown of communication. It also has to do with celebrating the abundance of life given to us. And it has to do with hope for a world when covenants are made and are maintained in justice and in harmony.

The cross stands at the center of God's saving activity. It marks the point where God has chosen to dwell in a special way in our world, "outside the gate" (Heb. 13:12). It is both the instrument of shame and the throne of glory. The blood of the cross is the source of our reconciliation and expiation.

Perhaps more than any other Christian symbol, the cross represents the paradoxes that cut across our experience. When conjoined to the symbol of the blood of Christ, all of those paradoxes
about power and weakness, glory and shame, achievement and
failure, life and death, come into sharp relief. The paradoxes and
the contradictions that map out the conflictual situations of our
world all find some illumination in the light of the cross.

A spirituality of the blood of the cross is committed to those who
suffer, and so feel the contradictions of life and society within their
bodies: how soon the promise of life is sapped by illness and death;
how often words of freedom turn into threats of enslavement; and
how commonly protestations of power are really expressions of
fear and insecurity. From the perspective of the cross, the misdirec-
tedness and venality of so much human ambition becomes clear.

But the blood of the cross is not just witness to the sinful and
sometimes barbarous nature of human activity; it is also a promise
of redemption—a redemption achieved by squarely facing the situations of violence and conflict in which we live, and by staying in
solidarity with those who struggle for a better world in those
situations. The cross is not just witness to humanity's capacity for
sin; it is a support for those who work for justice. It holds forth the
firm belief that suffering can be redemptive, can be turned from its
destructive tailspin to a spiral of solidarity in Christ and redemption of the enslaved.

The spirituality of the cup brings together the spirituality of the
covenant and cross. Gathered into the cup shared when Christians
gather are the sufferings and joys, the disappointments and the
hopes, the defeats and the victories of those who follow Jesus. As a
cup of blessing and a cup of suffering, the cup of the eucharist
offers comfort and hospitality to those who work for the reign of
God. It is a sign of solidarity among those who now struggle and
suffer, and presages the heavenly banquet when the fullness of that
reign will be revealed. The spirituality of the cup of the blood of
Christ reminds us that we have a Lord who has known our lives in
its many dimensions, a Lord who can appreciate our celebrations
of small successes, and can commiserate with our failings and
pain. By sharing that cup, we become in an important way the
living body of Christ, the presence of the living Lord in a world still
so much in need of his message.

By way of conclusion, a sketch of a form of commitment to a
spirituality of the blood of Christ might be helpful to give ex-

pression to the sentiments and ideals of this way of living out the gospel of Jesus Christ:

Redeemed by the blood of Christ, we strive to deepen our understanding of what God has done for us in this great act, and to allow it in turn to direct our mission and ministry. We do this by reflecting especially on three aspects of this great mystery: the blood of the covenant, the blood of the cross, and the blood of the cup.

In the blood of the new and everlasting covenant, we find the strength to build up and restore the many broken covenants that scar the human family. In the blood that speaks more eloquently than that of Abel, we work to establish communication and dialogue where isolation and hatred have taken root. In the blood of the covenant that will be fully revealed to us only in the kingdom of heaven, we struggle now for the justice that marks the presence of God among us.

In the blood of the cross we search for the redemptive moment in the sufferings of the world, and pledge ourselves to walk with those who pilgrimage through the somber valley of their affliction. We seek, too, beneath the cross, to learn of the power and wisdom of God among the poor and the weak. And in accepting the paradox of redemptive suffering through the blood of the cross, we grow in our obedience to the ways of God in our world.

In the blood of the cup, we commit ourselves to solidarity with those who suffer and hope for a better world. In our celebration of the eucharist and our sharing in the eucharistic cup, we build up the body of Christ for the work of the coming of the reign of God and its justice.

References

Two things seem obvious to me in writing a book on spirituality: a great many works influence the author, and footnotes are somewhat out of place. How to call attention to works that have influenced me in the writing of this book is something of a problem. What I have chosen to do is to cite works that are referred to in the body of this book, and also works that I have drawn from in a special way, works dealing directly with the content of this book.

In the latter category, I have learned much from two collections of essays that have tried to grapple with the same questions about a spirituality of the blood of Christ as I do here. The first collection is a three-volume set of proceedings of study weeks held on the theme of the theology of the blood of Christ at Saint Joseph's College, Rensselaer, Indiana, in 1957, 1960, and 1968. These were edited by Edwin G. Kaiser and are each entitled *Proceedings of the Precious Blood Study Week* (Rensselaer, Indiana: Precious Blood Institute, 1957, 1960, 1968), and will be referred to here as *Proceedings 1, 2, 3*.

The second collection also derives from study weeks, held in Rome, 1980–84, and has been published in four volumes (with a total of ten parts). The volumes are entitled, respectively, *Sangue e antropologia biblica; Sangue e antropologia biblica nella patristica; Sangue e antropologia nella letteratura cristiana;* and *Sangue e antropologia nella liturgia.* All were published by the Centro Studi Sanguis Christi in Rome. They will be cited here as *Atti*, followed by volume number, volume part, and page numbers.

Chapter 1: Roberto Gelio, "Il rito del sangue e l'identificazione del *negeph lemashit*," *Atti*, 1, II, 467–76; Francesco Vattioni, "L'Agnello Pasquale di Es 12, 1–14, *Atti*, 4, I, 229–322; Pietro Zerafa, "Il significato del sangue nella pasqua biblica," *Atti*, 1, II, 453–66.

Chapter 2: Francesco Vattioni, "Il sangue dell'alleanza (Es 24, 8)," *Atti*, 1, II, 497–514.

Chapter 3: Edward Siegman, "Blood in the Old Testament," *Proceedings* 1, 33–65; Rita Vivoli, "Il sangue nel Levitico," *Atti*, 4, I, 323–62.

Chapter 4: Massimo Baldacci, "Il ruolo del sangue nella teologia del peccato in Isaia," *Atti*, 4, I, 397–402; Mitchell Dahood, "'Sangue,' 'DM, Fenicio-Punico, Isaia 63, 2," *Atti*, 2, I, 155–56; Max Walz, *Why Is Thy Apparel Red?* (Carthagena, Ohio: Messenger Press, 1914); Johannes Baptist Metz, *Befreiendes Gedächtnis Jesu Christi* (Mainz: Matthias Grünewald Verlag, 1970).

Chapter 5: Giuseppe Gamba, "Il sudor di sangue di Gesú al monte degli Ulivi (Lc 22, 44)," *Atti*, 1, II, 689–714.

Chapter 6: Salvatore Panimolle, "Il valore salvifico della morte di Gesú negli scritti di Luca," *Atti*, 1, II, 661–74; Winfried Wermter, *Blut Christi: Kaufpreis unserer Erlösung* (Leutesdorf: Johannes Verlag, 1983).

Chapters 7 and 8: Barnabas Ahern, "The Fellowship of His Suffering," *Catholic Biblical Quarterly* 22 (1960) 1–32; Giovanni Deiana, "Il sangue in alcuni testi paolini," *Atti*, 3, II, 767–98; Romano Penna, "Il sangue di Cristo nelle lettere paoline," *Atti*, 1, II, 789–814; Kazimierz Romaniuk, "Il valore salvifico del sangue di Cristo nella teologia di San Paolo," *Atti*, 1, II, 771–88; Edward Siegman, "The Blood of Christ in Saint Paul's Soteriology," *Proceedings 2*, 11–35.

Chapter 9: Jacob Kremer, *Was an den Leiden Christi noch mangelt* (Bonn: Peter Hanstein Verlag, 1956).

Chapter 10: Antonio Cernuda, " 'Non da Sangui'—In mezzo all'incarnazione di Gv 1, 13.14," *Atti*, 4, II, 581–604; Settimio Cipriani, "Il sangue di Cristo in S. Giovanni," *Atti*, 1, II, 721–38; Stanislas Lyonnet, "Il sangue nella trafittura di Gesú: Gv 19, 31ss," *Atti*, 1, II, 739–44; Ignace de la Potterie, "Il costato trafitto di Gesú (Gv 19, 34)," *Atti*, 4, II, 625–60; Robert Siebeneck, "The Precious Blood and Saint John," *Proceedings 1*, 65–92.

Chapter 11: Charles Anderson, "Who Wrote 'The Epistle from Laodicea'?" *Journal of Biblical Literature* 85 (1966) 436–40; Herbert Braun, *An die Hebräer* (Tübingen: J. C. B. Mohr, 1984); Robert Jewett, *Letter to Pilgrims* (New York: Pilgrim Press, 1981); Ernst Käsemann, *Das wandernde Gottesvolk* (Göttingen: Vandenhoeck & Ruprecht, 1959); Albert Vanhoye, "Il sangue di Cristo nell'Epistola agli Ebrei," *Atti*, 1, II, 819–30.

Chapter 12: Ugo Vanni, "Il sangue nell'Apocalisse," *Atti*, 1, II, 865–84.

Index of Biblical References

139